Beechcraft Bonanza A36, Bonanza V35B, Bonanza F33A.

They Called Me 'Mr. Bonanza'

by

Larry A. Ball

Author of
Those Incomparable Bonanzas

Published by
McCormick-Armstrong Co., Incorporated
Publishing Division
1501 East Douglas Ave., Wichita, Kansas 67211

Library of Congress Card Catalog Number 90-063687

ISBN 0-911978-05-4

ACKNOWLEDGEMENT

The writer is indebted to many for the assistance
given over the years which made this book possible,
but in particular to Gib Urick, Ralph Harmon,
Dick Matson, and Bob Magness.

— Larry A. Ball

This book is dedicated to

- those who designed the Beechcraft Bonanza

- those who manufacture and fly it

- to Mrs. Olive Ann Beech — the first lady of aviation

- and especially to my wife, Linda, who stood by during those long hours of writing with good cheer and encouragement.

CONTENTS

PREFACE

My twin brother and I made model airplanes like most of the boys from that era, but we never dreamed of actually flying, even though we had relatives working at the airport, two of whom were pilots. We did have little paper Piper Cubs that "flew" in a paper box by strings attached to a control stick, courtesy of Piper Aircraft Corporation. Then one day in May, 1945, a neighbor boy biked out to the airport and paid $2.00 for a 15-minute ride in a Piper J-3 Cub. He came back with such enthusiasm for flying we soon found ourselves on our bicycles pedaling our way to the airport. My log book records a first flight of 15 minutes on May 12, 1945. Thus began a career of 45 years in the aviation business. I was 13 years old at the time. The $2.00 came from mowing four lawns with a hand powered reel mower.

The Tailspin Flying Club, 1945. From left to right, George Black, Ted Fisher, James Bird, Gary Ball, Tom Smyer, Bucky Taylor, Kenneth Smith, and Larry Ball.

Smyer Aircraft Sales and Service, Ponca City, Oklahoma, where I learned to fly, was the Piper Distributor for the state of Oklahoma. Tom Smyer was also a Dealer for Culver, Fairchild, and Stinson, so we had a good variety of airplanes to fly. During World War II, Ponca City was also the home of the Darr School of Aeronautics. Their task was to train British cadets in Stearman PT-17s, Vultee BT-13s, and North American AT-6s. Primary, Basic and Advanced training.

After the war the Darr facility was taken over by Piper Aircraft Corporation and turned into an assembly plant. To the north, between Ponca

Pre-war Taylorcraft — Ponca City, Oklahoma, 1947.

City and Wichita, set Arkansas City, Kansas. Fairchild had a plant there on a former Republic P-47 fighter training base. And, of course, in Wichita we had Beech, Cessna, Boeing, Culver, and Mooney. To the East in Coffeyville, Kansas, we had the Funk Airplane Company.

Piper shut down after two years of production and left. The Reconstruction Finance Corporation moved in. Suddenly, we had war planes of every possible description. Hundreds of them. They were flown in to be destroyed. There was security, of course. At night, we would climb the fence and go exploring in the bombers and fighters closest to the fence. It was great fun.

The last airplanes from the war effort to arrive were Fairchild AT-26s. These were bomber pilot trainers. Few people have seen this airplane. Fairchild had just begun production when the war ended. The forty or fifty airplanes that were flyable were flown directly from the Fairchild factory in the East to Ponca City. There they set for several years deteriorating in the sun and rain. They were made of wood. Their power plants were two in-line, inverted Ranger engines made by Fairchild. Finally a few of them were sold in South America and were flown away. The rest were scrapped.

Larry A. Ball with first flight instructor, Ted R. Fisher — Ponca City, Oklahoma, 1945.

Pre-war Culver Cadet, 1949.

Tom Smyer, 1950.

Employees of Smyer Aircraft Sales and Service, 1949. The hangar is a converted oil tank cover from Conoco Oil Company.

Pre-war Stinson 105 — Powered by a Continental 75 H.P. engine — Ponca City, Oklahoma, 1950.

Pre-war Fairchild — Ponca City, Oklahoma, 1949.

Pre-war Beechcraft Staggerwing — Ponca City Oklahoma, 1949. Note surplus military trainers in background.

Ryan PT 22 — A war surplus trainer — Ponca City, Oklahoma, 1949.

Pre-war Luscombe 8A. I air dropped bundles of newspapers to small towns around Arkansas City, Kansas, during two weeks in June, 1953, in a Luscombe 8A.

Pre-war Piper J-3 Cub — Ponca City, Oklahoma, 1945.

Our first post-war Piper J-3 Cub. Sign on side reads, "It's fun to fly a Piper Cub," 1946.

Cockpit enclosed Stearman PT-17 — Ponca City, Oklahoma, 1946.

Pre-war Aeronca 11AC Chief — Ponca City, Oklahoma, 1946.

Nearly new Grumman F6F Hellcat donated to local Garfield High School for shop use — Ponca City, Oklahoma, 1946.

Post-war Aeronca 7AC Champion. We had an Aeronca dealer at Ponca City, Oklahoma, for a short time — 1947.

C.M. McVay, our short lived Aeronca dealer, I think he sold one airplane — 1947.

7

Our first Piper PA-11 Cub — Ponca City, Oklahoma, July 9, 1947.

Pre-war Rearwin — Ponca City, Oklahoma, 1946.

Surplus Piper L-4 Grasshopper in civilian paint — Ponca City, Oklahoma, 1946.

War time Reconnaissance Taylorcraft — Ponca City, Oklahoma, 1946.

Ercoupe — Ponca City, Oklahoma, 1946.

Piper Cub L-4, in olive drab with a civilian stripe — Ponca City, Oklahoma, 1946.

Cessna UC-78 Bobcat. Years later, in Wichita, I got my twin engine rating in one of these. Terrible single-engine performance — Ponca City, Oklahoma, 1946.

Fairchild Primary Trainer with enclosed cockpits — 1946.

Lineup of surplus Stearman PT-17 primary trainers — Ponca City, Oklahoma. Many years later I attempted to make a summer living by crop dusting cotton in these airplanes out of Monroe, Louisiana. Fortunately for me, the boll weevils that year all died from thirst because of a drought. I didn't dust a single swath.

Our one salesman at Smyer Aircraft, Harold Moore
—1947.

Bill McMillan, Mechanic, Flight Instructor, Charter
Pilot for Smyer — 1950.

Pre-war Piper J-4 Cub — 1949. It was the first Cub to have side-by-side seating.

Pre-war Aeronca K. Two-place (barely), side-by-side seating. Power plant was a two cylinder Indian motor.

World War II Taylorcraft Training Glider waiting to be converted into an airplane — Ponca City, Oklahoma, 1947.

Me on the wing of a Vultee BT-13 — 1949. Tom Smyer purchased from war surplus many PT-17s, PT-19s, BT-13s, and AT-6s for resale.

Reconstruction Finance Corporation's military airplanes in storage at Ponca City Airport — 1949. The former Darr School of Aeronautics is in the lower left corner of the picture.

Reconstruction Finance Corporation at Ponca City — 1949. Front row consists of Observation Airplanes, North American P-51 Mustangs are a row back.

Vultee BT-13 Basic Trainers await their fate.

Beech AT-11 Bomber Trainers await the scrap heap.

A Fairchild AT-26. These airplanes were never used in service.

A ferry trip from Lock Haven, Pennsylvania, to Ponca City, Oklahoma, June 15, 1949.

Piper Clipper — 1949.

Piper's delivery hangar at Lock Haven — 1950.

Lock Haven was so covered with coal dust back then, every airplane had to be washed on delivery day.

Piper PA-12 Super Cruiser. I flew Serial No. 1 on November 2, 1947. Later I flew Charter in Super Cruisers.

1948 Aeronca 15AC Sedan. This aircraft was manufactured from 1948 thru 1951. A total of 561 were built. I had the pleasure of flying one out of Blackwell, Oklahoma.

1948 Cessna 170 — Wichita, Kansas.

1948 Cessna 140 — Wichita, Kansas. I flew pipe line patrol in one of these.

1952 Cessna 170B on the old Wichita Municipal Airport.

So we had a lot of airplanes around. We started working at the airport washing airplanes for flying time. A flying club was formed consisting of four presolo teenage boys. Later, we became line boys. I soloed on my 16th birthday, September 4, 1947, with 39 hours, 35 minutes of dual flying time. My next airport job was as a mechanics assistant, then charter pilot, and flight instructor. After two years of junior college at Northern Oklahoma Junior College in Tonkawa, Oklahoma, I decided I wanted to go out in the world and make some real money. Through an ad in *Trade-A-Plane* I applied for a crop dusting job. I was accepted within a few weeks by a Delta Airlines Captain who had a dusting operation on the side.

I took a bus to Jackson, Mississippi, to start my great adventure. He had a fleet of three Stearman PT-17s with high horsepower engines. As I recall, they were Lycoming 300 H.P. radials. He checked me out on spraying technic and we were ready for the season to start. After about a month in Jackson we relocated to Monroe, Louisiana, where the season traditionally started. By now I was beginning to have doubts about all this. I had noticed on the way down the heights and number of trees as we drove South. My previous recollection of aerial agriculture pest control was in the broad plains of Oklahoma and Kansas using spray planes at a height of eight feet. Here we would be dusting at a height of four feet with tall trees at the end of each small field. But I stayed on.

Then word began circulating among the duster pilots gathered in Monroe that there might not be a dusting season that summer. There had been a drought and it appeared the boll weevils all died from thirst.

About that time I noticed an ad in *Trade-A-Plane* for flight instructors. The Korean War was going full blast and the Air Force was asking civilian contractors to quickly set up training bases for Air Force Cadets, manned by civilian flight instructors. The ad I responded to was a school being set up by Southern Airways. I took a bus to Birmingham, Alabama, was interviewed, and hired. You were supposed to be at least 21 years old . . . I was only 19 . . . so I lied about my age. I went on to Bainbridge, Georgia, where the Southern Airways base was to be located. I began checking out in the North American AT-6G almost immediately. I lasted all of four flights before being washed out. I had flown Vultee BT-13s many times but never an AT-6G. Actually, two things happened to me. One, I was incompetent, and two, some of the boys started showing up from the crop dusting outfits, many of them former Air Force instructors or pilots. The boll weevils had died of thirst. These new guys knew the AT-6G. I didn't stand a chance.

Actually, it wouldn't have worked out anyway. Years later I bumped into two of my former colleagues at Lambert Field, St. Louis, Missouri. We were all draft age back then and assumed we would get deferments as Air Force instructors. They made the grade and still got drafted. Anyway, I sulked home and begged my Dad to fund me for my remaining two years of college at Oklahoma A&M. He did and I started school in two weeks. This had been the worst summer of my life. I graduated in June of 1953 and was drafted in October of that year. By the time I completed training, the shooting had stopped in Korea. I guess I accomplished something.

Me on the wing of a North American AT-6G — Bainbridge, Georgia, August 12, 1951.

The Boys of Summer — Bainbridge, Georgia, 1951.

Crash Duty off the approach end of the runway — Bainbridge, Georgia, 1951.

Reo Rudd and Larry Ball — Bainbridge, Georgia, 1951.

On the front porch of our boarding house — Bainbridge, Georgia, 1951. My two friends also got drafted.

With mom on Graduation Day from Oklahoma A&M — 1953.

Camp Chaffee, Arkansas — November, 1953.

Fort Hood, Texas — November, 1954.

After my discharge from the Army, I went immediately to Wichita with the idea of going to work for Cessna. Their products were closer to my Piper background. Neither Cessna nor Beech were hiring at the time so I took a temporary job at Boeing Airplane Company as a Methods Engineer. For the next 1.5 years I kept knocking on doors, Beech finally answered. I had called about an opening in the outside procurement department they had advertised in the *Wichita Eagle*. I had worked in procurement for Conoco Oil Company after college and before being drafted.

Roy Kuntz in Beech personnel had taken an interest in me. I was ready to do anything to get out of Boeing. It turned out there was an opening in Beech Customer Service. I was interviewed by Del Spillman and hired.

At Beech I served as Bonanza Customer Service Representative, Model 18 Modification Salesman, Assistant Sales Manager, Bonanza, Regional Manager, North Central Region, Assistant Sales Manager, Bonanza and Debonair, Sales Manager, Bonanza and Debonair, Program Manager, Bonanza, Beechcraft Hawker 125 Completion Center Manager, and finally, Program Manager, Bonanza and Baron. My last 15 years in the industry was as Vice President and General Manager of Indiana Beechcraft. During 1986 and 1987 I was also Vice President and General Manager of Ohio Aviation, Cleveland, Dayton, Cincinnati, and Hartzog Aviation, Rockford, Illinois.

Walter Beech with my predecessor, Colonel Roscoe Turner, President of Roscoe Turner Aeronautical Corporation — Indianapolis, Indiana, 1946.

Walter H. Beech and Olive Ann Beech inspect an early Beechcraft Bonanza 35 — March 21, 1947.

ABOUT MRS. BEECH

I worked for her for 25 years and never heard a cross word. There were plenty of rumors around the plant that she was difficult to work for, and if you ever got on her bad side, there was no recovery. I never saw any of this. She was always kind and considerate. We had a custom at Christmas time where she personally passed out all the year end checks. She always asked me the same thing, "What did you sell today, Mr. Ball?" I always hoped I'd have an answer. The first time I had lunch with her more or less one on one was when she invited me to lunch with her and the President of Stephens College, Columbia, Missouri. We had given Stephens a good deal on a Debonair demonstrator and he was in town to formally accept it. At that time we didn't have decent dining facilities at the factory so we had to go downtown. Let me tell you, I was nervous. When we finished lunch, I started to excuse myself to go check to be sure her driver was out front and she said, "Don't bother, Mr. Ball. If he is not out there, he doesn't work for me anymore." That's the strongest thing I ever heard her say in 25 years.

WHAT DOES A
FACTORY SALES MANAGER DO?

AT HEADQUARTERS

At the factory, there's a great variety of tasks. Easily taking first place would be escorting and entertaining visiting customers, prospects, distributors, and dealers. We also did flight demonstrations at the factory. And there were endless internal meetings. Factories love meetings. Speaking of meetings, a lot of time was spent preparing for the annual Dealer Sales Meetings.

We spent time with the press both on the ground and in the air doing pilot reports. We lectured in sales training sessions. At least in my case, spec'ing airplanes to keep the production line going was a significant task. We developed demonstration manuals for the field salesmen. I supervised as many as four factory salesmen. We devoted a lot of time working with Engineering on product changes. We made sales forecasts for manufacturing. We worked with Advertising on new layouts, with Styling on new exterior paint designs and new interiors. We worked with Quality Control and the Pricing Department.

We were responsible for comparison information with competing airplanes. I turned this into an art form on at least two occasions. Toward the end, I became disillusioned with this form of promotion. I began to believe all we were doing was advertising the other guy's product. The prospects were not believing us anyway, figuring the comparisons were bound to be rigged in our favor.

IN THE FIELD

Our job was to work with the field salesmen to improve their demonstration skills and to work with them on their product knowledge and prospects. We often became an excuse to "call again" because the factory expert was in town. We were also available to speak to civic organizations and flying clubs. It was a great life until I came upon my personal lifetime limit of nights on the road in motels and hotels.

BEECHCRAFT'S CURRENT SALES TRAINING PROGRAM

Beech Aircraft Corporation
P O Box 85
Wichita KS 67201-0085 USA

316 681 7111
Telex 71 203603

Beechcraft
A **Raytheon** Company

January 17, 1990
AB-90-3

INDIVIDUALLY ADDRESSED TO ALL BEECHCRAFT CORPORATE AND EXECUTIVE AVIATION CENTER
PRINCIPALS, SALES MANAGERS AND INTERNATIONAL DISTRIBUTORS AND DEALERS

SUBJECT: Professional Beechcraft Bonanza Salesman Award

The Professional Beechcraft Bonanza Salesman Award was initiated in 1977. The
program was initially offered only to the domestic U.S. sale force, but we are
pleased to announce the program is also being extended to the international sales
force as well at this time. The award has served as a motivating tool for more than
a decade in our collective efforts to maximize our Bonanza sales.

We are recommitting our efforts to this program and would like to review with you
the qualifications for a salesperson to receive the award:

1. Candidate has at least one year employment at a Beech Aviation
   Center/International Distributor or Dealer.

2. Candidate has demonstrated sufficient product knowledge and demonstration
   technique to a member of the King Air & Piston Product Marketing group.

3. Candidate has sold at least three (3) new Bonanzas (any model) in their
   marketing area.

4. Candidate has successfully completed the Professional Selling Skills III
   sales training course.

The award consists of a beautiful oak desk plaque, and highly stylized lapel pin,
for each qualifying salesperson and name recognition for each salesperson on the
master plaque at Beech corporate offices.

Now may be a good time to review with your sales force, the status of each
salesperson and determine what they need to qualify for this award.

Please contact the newest member of our product marketing team, Ken Stultz, or
myself for assistance and qualifying status. Ken will be administering the program.

We look forward to announcing the award winners at our next International Sales
Conference.

Sincerely,

Blair P. Sullivan
Manager
King Air & Piston Product Marketing

BPS/bm

27

Management team, which conceived and directed development of the Bonanza 36, are (from left) L.L. Pechin, Vice President-Manufacturing; John Pike, Program Manager-Bonanza Models; Larry Ball, Sales Manager-Bonanza Models; and James N. Lew, Vice President-Engineering.

Beechcraft Model 36 Bonanza.

Forward baggage space, Model 36 Bonanza.

Model 36 Bonanza introduction in the Walter H. Beech Hall — June, 1968. From left to right, Larry A. Ball (author), Linda Ball (author's wife who was four months' pregnant), Ed Muhlfeld (editor of *Flying Magazine*), and Archie Trammell (reporter for *Flying Magazine*).

MODEL 36 BONANZA

This was my airplane. I fought for it for four years. Cessna was killing us with the Cessna 206. It was finally approved, and we began splitting the cabin roof from the keel section, in effect moving the passengers and the engine ten inches farther forward. We needed a six place airplane — we needed an improved center of gravity envelope.

Our custom at that time was to take advance dealer orders on a new model. I had a problem with this policy on the Model 36. Due to slow sales that year, we had been building unsold V35As to keep the producton line going. We had twenty-four airplanes in storage at our plant in Salina, Kansas.

I felt we couldn't announce the new airplane and take orders, and at the same time liquidate the Salina inventory. I devised a scheme to begin production on one hundred airplanes. They would all be built to factory specifications and we would keep quiet about them. We would have a surprise Distributor Meeting during June, 1968. We wanted to have twenty-five units ready to deliver at the time of introduction, one unit for each Distributor. At the production line rate we had then, we had to spec out one hundred airplanes to have twenty-five completed.

At that time I worked for Tom Gillespie, Domestic Sales Manager. I approached him with the idea and he liked it. Now the job was for him to sell it to Wyman Henry, Vice President of Marketing, and Frank Hedrick, President. I thought the odds were against us. It had never been done before (and hasn't been done since). Tom Gillespie was kind of a fair-haired boy around Beech. He was the heir apparent and well liked. He sold the program! I could hardly believe it! A few weeks later Tom had a disagreement with Hedrick and left Beech for Lear Jet. I was certain our plan would get scrubbed with him gone. I'll probably never know, but I think Henry and Hedrick forgot about it. Tom Gillespie later joined Piper Aircraft as Vice President of Marketing.

The production line went almost solid with Model 36 Bonanzas. We closed Plant II to visitors. Meanwhile, we were gradually selling the V35As in Salina. We had a Dealer meeting at Beech in May of that year. They wanted to tour Plant II. I told the group we had some confidential military projects going on there and the plant was closed to the public. Their disappointment was all too evident, so we told them we would arrange a tour for the following morning. John Pike, Bonanza Program Manager, grabbed some guys early the next morning and they papered over the double doors and the rear windows. I don't believe anybody suspected anything — if they did I never heard about it.

As the A36s came off the production line, all that was done by production flight test was to run a gear check and top them off with fuel. They were then flown to Salina. All production flight testing was done there. When we got close to having twenty-five units completed, we sent the Distributors a telegram over Frank Hedrick's signature telling them to be in Wichita on a certain date and to bring their checkbooks. They would be taking home a new Beechcraft. The day before the meeting, we flew all the 36s back from Salina to Beech Field. It looked like a daisy chain of Bonanzas between Salina and Wichita.

The meeting was held in the Walter Beech Hall across the street from the main plant. We had four Model 36 Bonanzas in the hall, all covered with ceiling mounted shrouds, We moved the order department across the street complete with desks, file cabinets, order books, green eye shades and black arm bands. Walter Gunstream, then Domestic Sales Manager, gave the introduction. I gave a short thirty-minute presentation. At the proper time, the shrouds were lifted from the airplanes. There was an audible gasp from the audience. We started taking orders. We sold the twenty-five we had ready to go plus the seventy-five we had in the works. One hundred airplanes in one day. This was my place in the sun. It had never been done before at Beech.

Larry A. Ball and V-Tail at Beech Field — 1971.

THE V-TAIL

oy, did we struggle with this one. We had a limited center of gravity envelope, yet we wanted to keep the V-Tail for its distinctive look. We looked at building a bigger V-Tail, in fact we did a mock-up in the experimental shop. It was so big it looked like the airplane had grown a second set of wings. Of course, the ground balance would have been even worse than it already was, but we looked at it. To improve ground balance we looked at moving the landing gear back. No way. I talked to Ralph Harmon about this in 1965 while he was still with Mooney. We bumped into each other at a Flying Physicians Convention in Atlanta. He said "the Bonanza was too heavily integrated to change it."

When Leddy Greever, then Vice President of Domestic Sales, and I pushed the aft bulkhead back 19" in 1964 on the S35, we never dreamed this configuration would still be in production through 1982, 18 years later. It was a stop gap measure to us. After all, we were meeting annually at that time on a Bonanza replacement. But the tail end of the aircraft kept getting heavier and heavier. First the emergency locater transmitter, then lighter avionics forward of the C.G., then because the forward area was becoming full, avionics black boxes mounted aft of the rear bulkhead.

The last V35B we sold while I was at Indiana Beechcraft was to an airline pilot. The first thing he did was go home and calculate the envelope. He came back the next day to verify his results. I told him he was correct. He said, "you have got to be kidding."

My salesman, Mike Kelly, sold him a new A36 Bonanza the next day. I never inventoried another new V35B after that.

I had intended to do a section on the recent modifications to the V-Tail, but I can't improve on Beech's own Press Release. It follows:

Beech Aircraft Corporation
Public Relations Department
9709 E Central
Wichita KS 67201-0085
316 681 7602

Beechcraft
A **Raytheon** Company

News Release

Drew Steketee   (316) 681-7689
May 7, 1987

Beech Will Modify Many V-Tail Bonanzas

WICHITA, Kan. -- Beech Aircraft Corporation announced today that it will make a modification to the tails of approximately 5,300 of the 7,200 V-tail Bonanza aircraft still in service. V-tail Bonanzas were built between 1947 and 1982, and were certified in accordance with federal standards in effect at the time.

The affected V-tails will be modified at company expense. Beech will provide modification kits and a labor allowance for installation.

All V-tail Bonanzas have been operating at reduced speeds following issuance of a Beech Safety Communique on October 11, 1986, and a subsequent FAA Airworthiness Directive. The modification program will prepare affected aircraft to resume original operating speeds, as the company committed it would do in its Safety Communique. In addition to the modifications for those aircraft requiring them, resumption of normal V-tail operating speeds must await revision of the FAA's Airworthiness Directive issued in October 1986.

The approximately 1,900 V-tail Bonanzas not requiring modifications include the Model 35, A35 and B35 aircraft built between 1947 and 1950. Approximately 5,400 conventional-tail Bonanzas built since 1960 are not involved in the modification program.

-more-

34

The modification results from an extensive Beech testing program conducted in cooperation with the Federal Aviation Administration. During the testing, Beech discovered that the actual magnitude and distribution of aerodynamic forces on the tails of the affected aircraft differ from those used in the original design and certification process.

The resultant modifications include a small fuselage-mounted brace positioned over the stabilizer leading edge on C35 through V35B model Bonanzas built between 1951 and 1982. An additional external stabilizer reinforcement will be added to C35 through G35 model Bonanzas manufactured between 1951 and 1956.

Beech's exhaustive wind tunnel and flight tests found V-tail Bonanza flutter, handling, stability and control characteristics acceptable under FAA certification criteria.

Due to the age of the majority of the Bonanza fleet, Beech will only authorize work on aircraft with an airworthy fuselage tailcone and empennage. Each aircraft will be inspected at Beech's expense to assure airworthiness.

All affected models will get new safety placards and revisions to Pilot Operating Handbooks to assure that passenger and baggage loading practices adhere to weight and balance requirements. Changes will also include limitation of nose-down trim authority and, on C35 through G35 models, increased trim tab control cable diameter.

Modifications can be made by any Beech dealer, or by any qualified Airframe and Powerplant mechanic using kits, procedures and labor standards approved by Beech. A Beech service bulletin detailing the modification program will be mailed to V-tail owners of record in May.

-more-

The modifications restore the affected Bonanzas to their original design strength in relation to newly determined aerodynamic forces. However, no Bonanza has ever been shown to have failed because of these loads. Accident investigations indicate that Bonanza in-flight failures occur well above red line airspeed, generally as a result of loss of control of the aircraft.

Even with Beech's new modification, the V-tail Bonanza (like any other aircraft) is at risk of structural failure if operated beyond maximum G forces or red line speeds. The pilot remains responsible for maintaining the aircraft in an airworthy condition and operating it at a power, speed, weight and loading specified for his particular model as originally certified.

The company's extensive research and V-tail modification program are part of a commitment to Beechcraft owners by Beech, a subsidiary of Raytheon.

-050687-

May 7, 1987

BACKGROUND INFORMATION ON THE BEECH V-TAIL PROGRAM

Approximately 7,200 V-tail aircraft built by Beech between 1947 and 1982 are flying today. These range from the original Model 35 through the V35B. Some 5,400 additional Bonanzas (35-33, 35-A33, 35-B33, 35-C33, 35-C33A, E33, F33, G33, E33A, F33A, F33C, 36, A36, A36TC, and B36TC) were produced since 1960 with conventional tails.

The entire Bonanza line represents the longest production run of any aircraft in aviation history. Since the V-tail's application for the original Bonanza design in 1945-47, it has been a subject of much curiosity and technical specula-tion. Its design integrity has been verified on several occasions by Beech and government studies as conforming to federal standards for tail strength.

Beech volunteered its engineering assistance to the Federal Aviation Administra-tion in 1984 when the American Bonanza Society requested another verification of the V-tail Bonanza's structural integrity. A succession of studies beginning in the 1950s had previously confirmed the V-tail's conformance to federal standards. Government studies had also shown that structural accidents in the V-tail Bonanza almost always involved combinations of bad visibility, turbulence, thunderstorms, pilot inexperience and loss of control leading to overstressing the aircraft beyond its design strength.

-more-

The initial result of the latest FAA investigation was a 1985 report prepared by the Department of Transportation's Transportation Systems Center (TSC) which recommended that actual testing of the aircraft be performed to draw valid conclusions about the V-tail Bonanza. Beech volunteered to conduct a full investigation with the oversight and participation of the FAA in an effort to resolve all questions concerning the integrity of the V-tail, a goal which could only be accomplished with comprehensive wind tunnel, flight test and laboratory static test programs. The effort included wind tunnel testing of a full size V-tail and 146 test flights in a modified Bonanza aircraft during which some 11.5 million data points were gathered on each flight.

The three major parts of this program were:

1 - Wind tunnel tests to develop baseline data for flight and static testing. The wind tunnel tests were completed in the Lockheed tunnel at Marietta, Georgia, during March, 1986.

2 - Flight testing to measure aerodynamic loads, load distributions and flying qualities. The flight test research program was completed in November, 1986, and certification flight tests were completed in April, 1987.

3 - Static structural testing of the empennage for conditions based on flight and wind tunnel test aerodynamic load distributions. Structural testing was completed in April, 1987, for all V-tail models.

-more-

Flight Test Program

A Beechcraft Model K35 Bonanza with special instrumented tail structures was calibrated and flown through prescribed maneuvers. The flying qualities phase included testing at forward and aft centers of gravity, and also well beyond the aft c.g. limit.

The flight test program was divided into four phases as follows:

Flight Test Phase 1.   Aerodynamics and airloads with emphasis on pressure distributions in steady state conditions.

June, 1986 to August, 1986: 45 flights totaling 33.6 flight hours.

Flight Test Phase 2.   Aerodynamics and airloads with emphasis on local tail angle of attack / dynamic pressure in steady state conditions.

September, 1986: 17 flights totaling 10.1 flight hours.

Flight Test Phase 3.   Dynamic Loads - Symmetric maneuvers (Roller coasters), roll reversal and dynamic yaw maneuvers.

November, 1986: 4 flights totaling 2.9 flight hours.

Flight Test Phase 4.   Flying Qualities - Longitudinal and lateral/directional stability and control within the normal c.g. envelope and up to 3.6 inches behind the aft c.g. limit.

October, 1986 to November, 1986: 68 flights totaling 55.2 flight hours.

-more-

Outcome

Following loads development through wind tunnel and flight tests, numerous
static tests of the empennage and fuselage were conducted. It was determined
that modifications to the V-tail structure of the C35 through V35B models would
be required. Beech then designed the required modifications and structurally
tested them to certify the design to current FAA standards. Modification kits
are now certified and ready for installation.

To ensure a successful modification, Beech will inspect at its own expense the
area from the aft cabin bulkhead to the tail of any aircraft being modified.
The check will verify compliance with original specifications, Airworthiness
Directives and Service Bulletins. Corrosion or other structural weakness,
control cable or control circuitry problems, and other maintenance deficiencies
must be corrected at owner expense before the Beech-funded modification is
installed.

-050687-

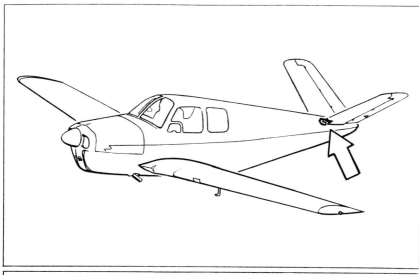

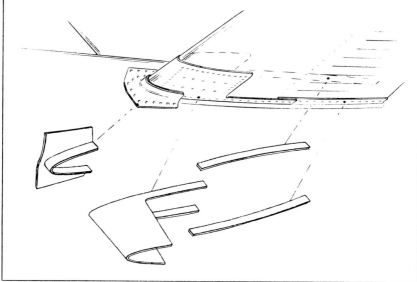

Aerobatic Bonanza with quick-release door — 1973.

AEROBATIC BONANZA

This program started out as a response to an interest on the part of the Japanese. We did some preliminary work and determined the idea was feasible, then the project was put on hold. The Japanese never placed their order (and still haven't). John Pike, who was Program Manager at the time, maintained an interest in developing the airplane. Frank Hedrick, then President of Beech, wanted a substantial order for the airplane before we spent any more money. As I recall, he wanted a commitment for seventy-five to one hundred airplanes.

I was in Atlanta, Georgia, on a sales trip when I got a phone call from Pike. He told me Hedrick would go with twenty-five airplanes and could I get the orders? I got on the telephone to our Distributors and sold twenty-five airplanes by the end of the day; all to domestic Distributors.

Bob Stone was the experimental test pilot who did the flight test work. Near the end of the program, he came into my office one day and invited me out for a flight. The airplane was still experimental so we had to wear parachutes. I wasn't too thrilled about that.

Bob and I climbed to altitude and he did a snap roll. Then he asked me to do a snap roll to the left, then to the right. Bob then said, "Now we will do a loop." I replied, no, we won't, let's go back home.

I got back to the office, still a little sick, and asked one of my assistants, Jack McFarlane, if he had flown aerobatics in the Navy. He had. I told him he was my designated aerobatic demonstration pilot. I never set foot in one again.

The airplane seems to have a life of its own. We have sold 179 units to date, with practically no promotion.

FROM FAA AIRCRAFT SPECIFICATION NO. 3A15:

ACROBATIC CATEGORY AIRPLANE

Maximum weight 2800 lb.

Flight maneuver load factor: Flaps up +6.0g, -3.0g

Center of gravity between Sta. 78.5 and 81.0

CAUTION: INVERTED FLIGHT IS PROHIBITED. Negative G flight is limited to 5 seconds or less as required to perform approved maneuvers. See acrobatic supplement to owners manual. ACROBATIC MANEUVERS WITH LANDING GEAR OR FLAPS EXTENDED ARE PROHIBITED.

Acrobatic boost pump must be on to perform the following:

Maneuver	Maximum Entry Speed (CAS)	
Chandelles, Lazy eights	152 m.p.h.	(132 knots)
Steep turns	165 m.p.h.	(143 knots)
Stalls and spins	Slow deceleration	

Maneuver	Recommended Entry Speed (CAS)	
Loop	190 m.p.h.	(165 knots)
Cuban 8	190 m.p.h.	(165 knots)
Immelmann	200 m.p.h.	(174 knots)
Barrel roll	150 m.p.h.	(130 knots)
Single snap roll	110 m.p.h.	(95 knots)
Vertical reversement	110 m.p.h.	(95 knots)
Split "S"	90 m.p.h.	(78 knots)

AIRSPEED LIMITATIONS (CAS)

Maximum landing gear extension speed	175 m.p.h.	(152 knots)
Maximum design maneuver speed	165 m.p.h.	(143 knots)

SPIN ENTRY: Stall with power off, flaps up, nose 15° above horizon. With full up elevator, apply full rudder in the direction of desired spin immediately prior to stall. IF AIRPLANE SPIRALS OR AIRSPEED EXCEEDS 130 M.P.H. IAS, INITIATE RECOVERY IMMEDIATELY.

NOTE: Keep ailerons neutral in entry and during spin.

SPIN RECOVERY: Simultaneously reverse rudder and elevator with ailerons neutral. Neutralize all controls as rotation stops.

In full view of pilot: Model E33C (CJ-23 through CJ-25); Model F33C (CJ-26 through CJ-30)

NOTE: CJ-1 through CJ-22 eligible for slow roll upon rework to install Kit 35-9012 or 33-921014 connector, 33-921015-1 reservoir assembly and 33-534088-1 placard which reads as follows:

> "This airplane must be operated in compliance with the operating limitations stated in the form of placards, markings and manuals. Refer to weight and balance data for loading instructions. Occupied seats must be in upright position during takeoff and landing. Altitude lost during stall recovery: 300 ft. No acrobatic maneuvers approved except those listed below."

(UTILITY AND ACROBATIC CATEGORY)

UTILITY CATEGORY AIRPLANE

Maximum weight: 3300 lb. (E33C); 3400 lb. (F33C)

Flight maneuver load factor: Flaps up 4.4g, Flaps down 2.0g

Maneuver	Maximum Entry Speed (CAS)	
Chandelles	152 m.p.h.	(132 knots)
Lazy eights	152 m.p.h.	(132 knots)
Steep turns	152 m.p.h.	(132 knots)
Stalls (except whip stalls)	Slow deceleration	

NOTE: Intentional spins prohibited.

AIRSPEED LIMITATIONS (CAS)

Maximum landing gear extension speed	175 m.p.h.	(152 knots)
Maximum design maneuver speed	152 m.p.h.	(132 knots)

VERTICAL INSTRUMENTS

This was a stoppable accident if everyone had been on their toes. I'm one of the guilty guys. The converging of events overtook us on this one. Three things happened: One, I was busy managing a five model Bonanza line-up in 1971; Two, a five member factory sales team; and Three, we introduced Program Management to Beech — Wichita from the Beech — Boulder Plant. Program Management was an Air Force concept that was adopted by Boulder because of our government production there. Anyway, the concept was moved to Wichita and to our civilian business.

John A. Pike (whom I later worked for) was a strong headed, Phi Beta Kappa type who blew in to Wichita with a progressive, 'let's get things done attitude.' He thought the new vertical instruments were great. The idea was to initially install them in the Bonanza and Baron. V.L. Gaston, who was Baron Sales Manager, and I were busy traveling and selling airplanes. We didn't pay enough attention to the new guy.

Before we knew it, we were deeply committed to a vertical instrument program.

In fact, as I recall, we had invested $1,000,000 before Gaston and I woke up. We were consulted of course, but we weren't paying much attention. These were decisions we had always made. Somehow, the Baron never wound up with vertical instruments. I think it was because of a lack of pilot visibility of the instruments with the throttles, mixture controls, and prop controls full forward.

The Bonanza, unfortunately, did. During their development, I left the Marketing Department to go into Program Management on June 29, 1969. The vertical instruments became my baby. I had real doubts about them; but I was determined to make them work for my new boss.

Every time I flew them (in the F33 N9005V, in my first book) I liked them less. We grow up looking at round dials, why do we need to read vertically? But that was a conceptual problem. The real problems were up ahead. We continued testing, and finally wound up ordering for the production line for the 1972 models.

The first big problem occurred on the production line during the summer of 1971. I wound up with an entire production line of Bonanzas with tachometers that didn't work. We were just about to start a two week plantwide summer shutdown, but I convinced Engineering to work during the shutdown to correct the problem. It turned out the probes to the engines were too short. They fixed that and we kept the line going.

First deliveries occurred in October, 1971. At first, it looked like they were okay. Meanwhile, I was moved to the Beechcraft Hawker 125 Completion Center Program for one year and did not have the time to monitor it closely. The fellow who replaced me obviously wasn't watching either. There were a few field checks made but nothing alarming turned up. What we later learned was that the airplanes were not being flown much. We were in the middle of the 1972 general aviation recession! Later in 1972 I was transferred back to the program just in time to discover we had real problems.

The transducers were the major problem but the instruments had their problems as well. And we had serious procurement problems.

I soon learned that there was no such thing as an inexpensive transducer. Finally all parties bit the bullet. After great expense, we dropped the program.

This was one of my most disappointing times at Beech Aircraft.

BONANZA REPLACEMENT

We used to meet yearly to discuss a Bonanza replacement. We never made any progress during that period. I would argue that it was unlikely we would destroy Bonanza tooling, so we were really talking about a second airplane. (I would later use the same argument on the Baron.) This went on for sixteen years . . . it got pretty boring.

TIGER TEAM

Beech had its first and only strike in June, 1969. Even before the strike, we had severe parts shortages. We were still bringing new people on board for training when the union walked out. The union was back in six weeks, but the problems that were there when they left had only grown worse.

In an effort to get the King Air line moving again, Beech established a "Tiger Team." The team consisted of a manager from each discipline, Program Management, Engineering, Scheduling, Procurement, Planning, Quality Control, and Manhours Control. The team had virtually unlimited powers to get things done and get the production lines moving again. It seemed to be working for the King Air line so management decided to do the same thing for the Bonanza and Baron line. I was to head that team. It was wild. To this day I don't know how much good we actually did. We had Engineering write a lot of deviations so we could, where possible, use Baron parts on Bonanzas and vice versa. We were essentially high level expeditors.

The one humorous thing I remember about all this was my procurement counterpart, Vern Eckels, driving to Wichita Mid-Continent Airport in his convertible to pick up a three bladed propeller for a Bonanza. Since they come assembled, they can be a little difficult to transport. His convertible was ideal, however, with the top down.

But here he was after five o'clock (all top management was gone) trying to drive through the West Gate at Beech. Normally, all component shipments go through Shipping — Receiving and Quality Control. We were bypassing those departments. The West Gate had a particularly obnoxious guard who was difficult to get by in the best of times, but old Vern talked his way in that night, with the three bladed prop sticking out of his back seat, by threatening to call Hedrick.

After four months it was apparent we were encountering diminishing returns. Also, the workers were starting to program overtime as a standard benefit. We shut it down after six months.

AIRPORT SURVEY

Shortly after Wyman Henry joined the company in 1959, he asked Lou Bellanger and I to survey every airport in Kansas. Wyman's objective was to locate possible locations for Beech Dealerships. I thought I knew what we would find, but Wyman was new to the industry, and he wanted an actual survey. I liked him, and besides, it might be fun. We drew up a questionnaire to be filled out for every airport operator in the state. Lou and I started out on a journey that was to last nearly two months. We obviously had some interruptions, or it could have been done a little sooner.

Our mode of transportation was a Bonanza from the transportation pool known affectionately as old R-1. In fact, as I recall, it had that painted on its cowling. R-1 was the first of the Model 35s that were rebuilt in 1951 (there were only thirteen Model 35s rebuilt, see my first book, pages 188 and 189). Its actual serial number was D-25. We started our trip on June 15, 1959. I won't list all the places we hit, but we did visit every strip in Kansas. Wyman didn't want anyone to know it was Beech who was making the survey, so we adopted a fictitious survey company name. We even surveyed strips where you had to telephone somebody in town to come out to the airport.

Lou was from Michigan. Apparently they don't have chiggers there. He got the first infestation of his life in Dodge City, Kansas. He got bitten really bad. He was still muttering about them when we completed the survey.

We gave Wyman the results. As expected by me, every airport that was large enough to conceivably support a fixed base operator already had a Piper or Cessna Dealer. None of these airports could support two dealerships. There were no holes. Later, we did briefly establish a dealership at Garden City, Kansas, but it was owned and controlled by United Beechcraft in Wichita. It didn't last long. Years later I encountered a similar situation in Cleveland, Ohio.

Old R-1, the first rebuilt Model 35.

NAME CHANGE

I didn't hear about it until the eleventh hour. I think our advertising agency and our own Advertising Department deliberatly kept me in the dark. The wanted the Debonairs to be called Bonanzas in 1968. Something about getting more advertising for our money by promoting only one name. I was against it when I finally heard about it. Hedrick was on my side. That was about the only support I had. Then he crumbled. I lost. By the name change we managed to confuse control towers around the world for months. There still may be confusion.

WING TIP TANKS AND THE THREE-BLADE PROPELLER

We learned very early not to put these two options together. It seems the full tip tanks (Brittain) stiffened the wing. Engine vibrations that normally dissipated off the wing tips came back into the cabin, especially with the three-blade propeller installed. We had at least two pilots turn back to Beech Field after takeoff — fearing they were having engine problems. We soon had a notation in our Bonanza price list that you could have one of the options but not both.

REGIONAL MANAGERS

We all have them. I was one for a year. Back in the 50s and 60s they might have made sense. We had closed territories then and the Regional Managers often acted as the judge, jury, and prosecutor in establishing infringement fees.

After the Justice Department stepped in the late 60s with a restraining order the only solid reason for having Regional Managers ceased to exist. Any important decisions are made at the factory. Yet we still have them. I guess we are copying the automobile companies.

MARKETING GURU

In the 1960s we had a Market Research Director who was something else. Hank Ryan and I argued about many things, but I remember two occasions very vividly. He was doing all the forecasting for my boss, Leddy Greever. He began consistently saying we will be selling fewer Bonanzas next year. So we built fewer, and sure enough, we sold fewer.

I had learned a trick from a former boss. Paul Allen was my boss while I was in Customer Service. I noticed when he didn't like what some other department was doing for him, he would duplicate the function in his own department. I went over to the Print Shop and had them print official looking forecasting forms for me — forms that looked much better and more official than what Hank was using. I started doing my own forecasting on the Bonanza and Debonair. It had an effect on Greever, the production rates stopped falling.

The other occasion occurred in Amarillo, Texas. Hank and I had gone down there with the Service Clinic to hold, for lack of a better term, what we called a Super Service Clinic. It consisted of the usual Clinic, plus lectures in the evenings, plus flight checks in the owner's airplanes. At the end of the week Hank told me, "The Bonanza is perfect as it is, all these people love it." I replied, "Of course they do, but you didn't talk to a single Commanche or Cessna 210 owner the whole time you've been down here."

BONANZA/BONANZA

During the mid 60s, our ad agency and the Beech Advertising Department dreamed up a promotion called Bonanza/Bonanza. It was a sweepstakes offering free Bonanza flying time. All you had to do to enter was fill out a form at your local Beech Dealership and mail it to sweepstakes headquarters. The prizes were:

    1 — two weeks use of a new Bonanza
    5 — weekend use of a new Bonanza
    20 — one hour of flight in a new Bonanza

All expenses were paid. The idea was to expose and sell Bonanzas. My department was put in charge of Bonanza/Bonanza. We spent the better part of the summer administering this program, moving Bonanzas around, and checking out winners. After the promotion was complete, I did an intensive audit of what we had accomplished. It turned out no airplanes were sold. For all the money and work we accomplished nothing. People who enter sweepstakes aren't the same people who can afford to own and operate a new Bonanza.

I wrote a very critical memo to Beech Management on Bonanza/Bonanza, recommending it not be continued. A year after I left for Indiana Beechcraft, they tried it again.

EVENING WITH BEECHCRAFT

Also in the mid 60s, Jerry Warner, who worked for me at the time, developed an idea I had only been thinking about. Actually, we both wound up working on it. Essentially, this program involved having the dealers who wanted to participate send us a list of prospects they wanted to influence. We would send them an invitation direct from the factory to attend an "Evening with Beechcraft." This promotion involved a sit-down dinner, a one hour slide presentation on the Bonanzas, and usually a Bonanza travel or demonstration film. I had four guys working for me at the time. All five of us began to put on these shows.

We blanketed the country, holding fifty 'Evenings With Beechcraft.' The more of these I conducted, the greater my doubts became. We had very little success, it was expensive (Beech picked up the dinner and liquor tab), and it was keeping us from being on the road selling one on one. I concluded that people who go to free dinners aren't the same people who can afford to own and operate a new Bonanza.

The company is still using this program.

Bonanza Sales Team, 1965. From left to right, Alan Wherry, next to him, Larry Long, Larry A. Ball, Jerry Warner, Jack McFarlane.

Checking out a Bonanza/Bonanza winner in Atlanta, Georgia. His total time was 90 hours in a Cessna 152.

Winner and family.

T.V. ADS

We believed for years that television wasn't the place to put our advertising dollars. That was the conventional wisdom in the entire industry. In the mid 70s Beech decided to test that theory. Some professional one minute spots were filmed on the West Coast, one on the Baron and one on the King Air. They were good. Since this was a factory sponsored promotion, Beech elected to only use markets controlled by factory owned stores. Two locations were selected, Indiana Beechcraft, a corporate franchise, and Beechcraft west, Fresno, California, an executive franchise.

A team came to town from Beech and their ad agency with the films, information packets, and questionnaires. Our telephone number would be shown at the end of the spots as the place to call for additional information. All employees were shown the spots, how to answer the telephone, and how to fill out the questionnaire. A lot of work went into this promotion. It ran for 90 days. The results were dismal in the Indiana market. They were even worse in the Fresno market. Most of the calls were from kids or guys in bars. The conventional wisdom was correct.

TRAVEL ANALYSIS

Piper, Beech and Cessna have all played with this over the years. It comes in two forms, a detailed study of the prospective company's travel requirements, or a hypothetical trip compared with other modes of transportation. I have never seen either method work.

I remember one of our salesmen, Lou Belanger, spending more than a year working with Cargill in Minneapolis, Minnesota, making numerous trips, gathering countless data not limited to but including airline ticket carbons, itineraries, frequency of travel, etc. He finally put together a presentation and flew back up there. They didn't buy. Years later, long after poor Lou had left Beech and the industry, they did get into corporate aviation, though not with our product.

I saw the same thing happen to a salesman in St. Louis, Missouri, with Brown Shoe Company. Years later they bought, but not our product. We had a salesman at the factory who worked two years on travel analysis all over the country. He was considered our National Accounts Executive. No sales. I don't know how he kept his sanity. One of the last King Airs I sold here in Indianapolis was to P.R. Mallory Company. The Manager of the Flight Department reported he wanted me to do a travel analysis. I politely said no. They bought anyway.

If the desire and money are not there for the customer, and the salesman can't make his product sizzle, no amount of analysis is going to get the job done.

ANNUAL SALES MEETINGS

We had four kinds while I was at Beech:

Regional Meetings
Wichita Meetings
Sales Spectaculars
NBAA Meetings

I don't remember having a favorite in the four. The meetings were held in Wichita until Wyman L. Henry came on board from White Motor Company. He and Hedrick were old friends. Frank brought him to Beech to strengthen our marketing effort. Anyway, it was soon after he joined us we started doing Regional Meetings. I think the idea was to take up less of the salesmen's time by going to them rather than having everybody come to Wichita.

All of the annual sales meetings understandably took a lot of preparation. It seemed like we would just finish one when we would have to start preparing for the next one, or at the very least, start thinking about it. At 90 days before the event, we really got serious.

REGIONAL MEETINGS

Wyman held the first regional event in 1964. As I recall, we hit eight locations around the country. The downside of regional meetings was considerable. Logistics suddenly became a problem. Reliability of the audio system became a problem. Control of the environment became a problem.

We had one meeting in Oakland, California, where a high school band was meeting next door. They started playing in the middle of my Debonair presentation. I just raised my voice and worked it into my talk.

It worked the other way also. Our Sales Manager on the Queen Air was Marvin Small. He didn't hear well so he talked real loud. He was also the company clown. At least twice during the regionals someone from a meeting next door would come over and ask us to hold it down, but we had fun. By the time one of these regional tours was over, we could give each other's presentation, we had heard them so much. (Wyman wouldn't let us leave the room during someone else's presentation.) I actually suggested that once for the novelty of it.

On the very first of these tours, I introduced the new, 1964 S35 Bonanza. We came up with a unique method to show the many changes we had made. I "built" the airplane on a velcro board in front of the dealers and distributors. I put on the new stinger tail cone, put six seats in the airplane and then put the new Continental IO-520-B engine in the airplane and then cowled it. The audience loved it. Walter Gunstream said it was the finest product presentation he had ever seen.

Larry A. Ball during 1964 presentation of S35 Bonanza in Philadelphia.

Marvin Small as "The Music Man" with Mrs. Olive Ann Beech, 1967 Sales Spectacular.

WICHITA MEETINGS

The last few years I was at Beech the meetings had moved back to Wichita. I remember one in particular. I had worked hard on a Bonanza presentation that incorporated the entire Bonanza history leading up to the new model. After rehearsal Leddy Greever called me over and told me not to use it — too much history. Go work up a new presentation. I only had two days before the meeting would start. I stayed home the next two days and worked on nothing else. There wasn't time to completely script a presentation. All I had time to do was cue it, the rest would be ad lib. Leddy loved it! Imagine my surprise 15 years later when C. Don Cary got on stage and gave virtually the same presentation. By then of course, Leddy Greever and I were both gone — but what a surprise!

Over the years the best presentation of all was done by Marvin Small, Manager of King Air Sales. His presentation used "The Music Man" as its theme. In the middle of his talk he had a high school marching band parade through the Walter Beech Hall. He got a standing ovation during the show. It wasn't till many years later I learned the extent of his efforts. From a mutual friend I learned that Marvin had flown to Indianapolis from Wichita on at least one occasion, and maybe more, to catch "The Music Man," which was playing at Starlight Musicals.

SALES SPECTACULARS

This type of meeting started in 1966 and ended with the 1968 meeting. I look back on it now as the "silly" season. They were expensive. Nobody will ever know how expensive they were because so much was off the budget. We would hire song and dance people out of New York City to showcase the production. I suspect they did trade shows all the time but I never knew that for certain. At this first spectacular the director asked all of us if there was anything special we did or anything special about us. Either I or Russ Rising told him I had an identical twin brother. My act was born!

I was introducing the new 1966 V35 Bonanza and C33A Debonair that year. At the end of my slide presentation the stage curtain was drawn. There stood two outhouse-like boxes with doors. One was marked "Debonair," the other "Bonanza." My twin brother Gary was already inside the one marked Debonair, dressed in white tie and tails, the costume symbolizing Debonair. The cowboy outfit I had on all through my presentation was a loose reference to the T.V. show "Bonanza." (I didn't think this up.) My outfit was made by a costume shop in Hollywood. It was supposed to look like the outfit Lee Marvin wore in "Cat Ballou." They didn't get close.

Anyway, the girls put me in the box marked Bonanza, closed the door, sprinkled magic sparkle dust, muttered a few magic words, said they were about to perform a miracle, opened the Debonair door, and Gary stepped out.

Left: Gary Ball; Right: Larry Ball. 1966 Sales Spectacular.

The roar of the crowd was unbelievable. We had fooled 95% of the audience. They actually thought I had been able to change clothes and slip into that other box in just a few seconds.

Then the girls sprinkled more magic sparkle dust, opened the Bonanza door, and I stepped out. The crowd roared again. Gary was scared stiff. He had one line to give and barely got it out in a tremulous voice. Earlier, I had considered doing the box trick first then let him do half my presentation. Thank God, I didn't do that. The audience loved the box trick. They talked about it in Dealer meetings for years.

For the 1967 Sales Spectacular I got hit in the face with a pie and then had a change of costume to white tails. In 1968 the girls tore my clothes off at the opening, revealing me in a gold lame suit. I guess those were my salad days.

NBAA MEETINGS

I only attended these as an observer since I had long ago taken over Indiana Beechcraft. I have mixed emotions about hitch hiking on the NBAA. It's my perception it tends to dilute the Beech Meeting. On the other hand, it does have the advantage of combining two meetings at one time and place.

Jim Yarnell, Manager of Advertising, in the 1966 Sales Spectacular. He had just jumped through the *Time* magazine cover.

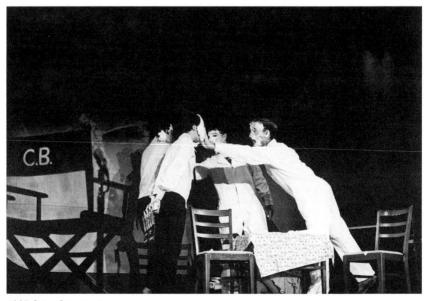

1967 Sales Spectacular.

1967 Sales Spectacular.

1968 Sales Spectacular.

From left to right: father, wife, mother and author at the 1968 Beechcraft Sales Spectacular. Biplane in background is a Travel Air.

Their job done, the girls are leaving to return to New York City.

FROM SALES MANAGER
TO PROGRAM MANAGER

Shortly after hosting the first annual meeting of the American Bonanza Society on June 26, 1969, in the Walter H. Beech Hall, I left Marketing for Program Management. My reasons for leaving Marketing were many. I had the feeling that I had been everywhere in the United States at least three times. I had a new wife and two years later my first child. I had managed to pick up a scary load of ice over the Allegheny Mountains between Pittsburgh and Rochester, New York. I lost all throttle control in a Turbocharged Bonanza in Banning Pass, California. I demonstrated to a prospect in Florida who got on board the airplane at high noon with beer on his breath. It turned out I had demonstrated to him ten years earlier. He had beer on his breath then. He was still flying a Cessna 182. I decided it was time to get out.

Program Management at that time was officed next to Marketing. I would just have to move a few offices East. I knew John Pike, who was currently Program Manager, Bonanzas and Barons, was being promoted to Director of Program Management. I talked it over with my wife, Linda. She was delighted with the idea that if I got the job, I would be staying home. I approached Pike the next week and got the job.

I'm told the Air Force insisted on Program Management after having worked with a company that used that approach. It may have worked for the Air Force, but I'm convinced it has no place in the commercial end of the business. We were like a fifth wheel. The people you work with: Engineering, Quality Control, Procurement, Marketing, Planning, Manhours Control, all have their own bosses, and you can't work for two bosses. It was not a very satisfying four years.

At least I wasn't traveling. I did learn about manhours control, cost control, and scheduling, for whatever that was worth. It was no wonder I jumped at the chance to take over Indiana Beechcraft.

Larry Ball and Miss Bonanza 1968.

Board of Directors, American Bonanza Society, with guests, tour Beechcraft — June 29, 1968.

Dr. B.J. McClanahan (right) discussing with me the unusually large attendance at the First American Bonanza Society Meeting — June 26-29, 1969.

First Annual American Bonanza Society Meeting — Wichita, Kansas, June 26-29, 1969.

BEECHCRAFT HAWKER 125 PROGRAM

We had just received our first jet a few days earlier. I was sitting in my office one day minding my own business when John Pike walked in and said I was his new Beechcraft Hawker 125 Completion Center Manager. I soon learned what a drill this was going to be. The next day Russ Rising, Vice President for Corporate Planning, called me to his office and gave me a big file on the jet he had been keeping for Hedrick. I spent a day going through the file. I'm sure there were some signed agreements somewhere but I never saw them. From the file it appeared the trips to England that Hedrick and George Humphrey, Executive Vice President, had been taking, consisted mostly of photo opportunities and hand shakes. I had very little to go on.

Engineering had been on the project for some time before I joined the team. We had purchased the cabin portion of the fuselage for a mockup several months earlier. Engineering had been working on the cabin interior and instrument panel layout in the mockup. They had also managed to spend several million dollars. I never completely believed in mockups. They are handy, but when you're done with them, they usually become junk. By using an airplane for this kind of work, you have something useful and of value when you're done.

We received the airplanes "green." I think that word was used because of the color of the exposed interior primer. Hawker would install a ferry kit to fly the airplanes over here. The kit consisted of just enough instruments and avionics to make the trip. Upon arrival, we would immediately remove the kit and ship it back to England for use in another airplane.

We assumed the payroll of the Hawker Service Organization in this country. Their people didn't hesitate to tell us that we might be paying them, but their hearts belonged to Hawker Siddeley. Owners of the Hawker 125 also resented us being in the loop. Our completion center was in competition with several well established completion centers around the country. It was tough competition because we were never able to completely free ourselves from the constraints of working out of a factory. Policies and procedures are quite different between a factory and a completion center.

After a while, I got the feeling the program was wrong philosophically, economically, politically, and geographically. Finally the day came when, for some reason, the second airplane wasn't coming from England. There was some high-level management disagreement. I asked John Pike to let me close the center — we didn't have any work. Pike asked George Humphrey. Humphrey said, "You will close it when I tell you to." We closed it anyway and I went back to my old job on the Bonanzas and Barons. I had the Completion Center for one year. I lost ten pounds. The Beechcraft Hawker Program was hard on everybody. George Humphrey had a heart attack and died. Lloyd Harris, who we inherited from Hawker, did not survive open heart surgery and died on the operating table. One man became an alcoholic. George Link, who had replaced me as Bonanza and Baron Program Manager, had a nervous breakdown and simply disappeared. What a summer. The disagreement between Beech and Hawker was later resolved. The center was reopened under Bruce Addington. It operated through 1975 and completed thirty-five airplanes. Sales were never good, so Hedrick bought out our contract with Hawker and the Completion Center finally closed for good.

Here is the only Beechcraft Hawker 125-400 completed while I ran the Completion Center.

Beechcraft Hawker 125.

Beechcraft Hawker 125.

Beechcraft Hawker 125.

Beechcraft Hawker 125.

The Beechcraft Hawker 125-600 replaced the 125-400. It was a stretched version with more power.

G33 Bonanza.

THE G33 BONANZA

About 1971, while I was Bonanza Program Manager, some in Beech Marketing got the idea we needed a lower priced Bonanza in our product line. A request was made to Engineering to look into it.

They came back with a proposal to put the Continental IO-470-N engine in the F33A Bonanza. They proposed replacing the high stability wing tips with old curved tips last used on the 1967 C33A. There was supposed to be a small savings in the bill of materials with the change in engines and a small savings in manhours with the change in wing tips. I argued strenuously against the proposal, pointing out it would make more sense to simply policy price the F33A. Continental was not even building the IO-470-N at that time. It was last used in the 1963 P35 Bonanza. I argued at several meetings, but in the end, I lost out.

As so often happens when Marketing thinks they want something, and Engineering is willing to provide it, Manufacturing usually loses out. Continental Motors very reluctantly agreed to build the engine again if we would order a minimum of fifty engines.

We received the first engine and installed it in the prototype. I remembered from past experience that it was not as smooth as the IO-520-B. Such proved to be the case with the fifty new engines. The engine mounts we were planning to use had to be discarded and replaced by the more expensive Lord mounts. There went the difference in the bill of materials.

The manhour savings were never realized, so we wound up building an airplane that cost as much as an F33A but lacked the performance. We only built the original fifty airplanes. The final irony of the program was that when I got to Indiana Beechcraft on March 4, 1973, I inherited the last two G33s in Dealer inventory. One was sold by my predecessor to our Dealer in Elkart who, in turn, sold it to a local Volkswagen Dealer.

The man called to tell me the engine was making metal. He was mad. An overhaul wouldn't do. He wanted a new engine. I called Continental and Beech, no engines. The fifty units were all that were built. United Beechcraft in Wichita, Kansas had the only G33 in Dealer inventory. I called my customer to see if he would be willing to swap engines. He was. So I reluctantly took United's G33 off their hands and made the swap. He must have been satisfied. I never heard from him again. We overhauled his original engine and put it in the second G33. Later that year I sold that unit to a Beech Dealer in Little Rock, Arkansas.

Looking back at the program I have to say "GEE why did we do it?" Years later, in 1987, we finally did policy price the F33A.

THE WIDE BARON

I bring this up only because it was part of the reason I left the Beech factory. Around 1970, while in Program Management, I proposed widening the Baron. We had the narrowest cabin of all the twins on the market at that time.

I'm sure Ralph Harmon felt 42" was about right in 1944, (I talked to him about this recently), but today people are a lot bigger. I wanted to widen the Baron and later the Bonanza. Jimmy Lew, then Vice President of Engineering, had $10,000 of pocket money we could work with. There was no management approval, we just did it. To show the concept, we took a model 58 mockup and cut it in half, right down the middle. Then we plugged it. I believe we used a 6" plug, but our proposal allowed for options of 4" to 8". It made for a really neat cabin. You could enter through the double doors and ease your way up front. We actually had a small aisle.

We showed it to management and later to a group of Distributor Principals. A vote was taken on this and other proposed model changes to the Bonanza and Baron. The wide-bodied Baron won out handily. In spite of this, management refused to endorse the proposal. I think my chief antagonist was Roy McGregor, then Vice President of Marketing. He didn't seem to like anything I did. The only reason I was ever given for the turn down was, "We did that once and it was called the Twin Bonanza." Nonsense! The carry thru structure, the landing gear, the Power Plants, the size and weight were all dramatically different.

I decided after that experience that I had minimum influence on product development. The other experience occurred a year later. John Pike, my boss at the time, and I talked Frank Hedrick into holding the Annual Sales Meeting downtown at Century II, a local convention center, rather than the cramped Walter Beech Hall. The meeting was such a success I became interested in selling again. I had been at Beech so long I couldn't afford to walk away from my benefits, so it would have to be with a company in Beech Holdings, a wholly owned subsidiary. I picked Denver Beechcraft, but Stewart Ayton, who was the President of Beech Holdings, asked me to take over Indiana Beechcraft. I told him I didn't want to run anything, I just wanted to sell. He said I could do both. He was partly right.

At Indiana Beechcraft — 1987.

INDIANA BEECHCRAFT

This was an ideal company for me to take over. It was small, with 64 employees, and was modestly profitable. We started out with $35,000 profit in 1972 and the company grew to $1,800,000 in profit in 1975. We became the world leader in the Beechcraft parts business. Line service grew to become a significant contributor to profit. One year I had $400,000 profit in line alone. After that year, I expected every year to be that good. Aircraft sales were usually good. We never were able to grow the service shop, but it was marginally profitable. The only drawback was the corporate headquarters. The building was put up in 1961, so it was hardly state-of-the-art.

BEECHCRAFT AERO CLUB

We gave this a hard four-year try. We lost a lot of money. I never knew how much because we commingled this activity with a charter operation, where we were also losing money. We were using brand new Beechcraft Skippers, which cost us $46,000 each. We were charging the highest rate per hour possible for our market, and we were still taking a beating. Finally, in the last year of operation, I personally took control of the Aero Club and really began crunching expenses. I couldn't make it play. We could afford this type of loss while we were selling a lot of King Airs, but this was 1982, and we were in a real general aviation slump. I closed it down. This was the end of my contribution to the general aviation community in Indianapolis. We might have broken even with some old, restored Beechcraft Sports, but not with new, $46,000 a copy Skippers.

CHARTER OPERATIONS

We started this up at about the same time we started the Aero Club. Talk about a double folly. We were using customer King Airs on lease backs, and our own Model 58 Baron. I learned later at Ohio Aviation that there must be a critical mass you have to reach in charter to be profitable. The Ohio charter department was at least breaking even or making a small profit — they had reached the critical mass of volume, we never got there in Indiana. I shut this activity down also. To me the main advantage of a charter operation in a Beechcraft franchise is having the pilot pool on your payroll. That way your salesmen can devote nearly 100% of their time selling instead of moving airplanes around.

The above two "experiments" cost me $500,000 in four years.

OHIO AVIATION

During 1985 I was asked by my boss at that time, Ernie Strum, to take over Ohio Aviation. The company had facilities in Dayton, Cleveland, and Cincinnati. I initially resisted. Hal Spragins, the man I was replacing, was taking over Hangar One. He convinced me I really had no choice if that's what Beech Holdings wanted me to do. My reluctance was based on a long-held belief in strong local management. I did not favor absentee management. But I accepted the challenge. All three companies were unique.

Dayton was the biggest, and most like Indiana. Getting it profitable simply boiled down to applying the same principles we had used at Indiana. Cost control, including payroll control, plus eliminating some old spanish customs, did the job. We also did manage to create synergy between Indianapolis and Dayton. Cleveland was the most difficult challenge. The more time I spent there, the more I became convinced it was just not doable. I was losing between $300,000 and $500,000 a year with no end in sight. I came to the conclusion we were the number two operator on the number three airport, Cayahoga County Airport. Several times I was there all afternoon and didn't see a fuel truck move, ours or the competition.

My predecessor had planned for a $1,000,000 expansion to improve business. I cancelled that. The planned expansion reminded me of an old World War II story.

It was said that after we left the South Pacific Area the natives, on one island built a make shift air strip and put a bamboo airplane on it in an effort to lure our planes back. I felt that was what we were about to do in Cleveland.

I closed the Avionics Shop, which helped a little, but we were still losing big money. Eventually, I convinced Management we should pull out of Cleveland. We sold the place and worked that area out of Columbus, Ohio.

Cincinnati was unique too. We had just spent $1,800,000 to expand and modernize our facility. The plan had been to virtually duplicate what we had in Dayton, only 95 miles away. With the general aviation recession getting deeper, I scrapped that plan. Our fuel sales were great, we had the best facility and best location on the airport, but the Parts Department and the Service Department were losing money. On top of that, they were actually at times competing with Dayton. I shut those two departments down and Cincinnati instantly became a cash cow.

HARTZOG AVIATION

They asked me to take over this Rockford, Illinois, company about a year after I acquired the Ohio companies. I didn't get to work much with Hartzog because I retired shortly thereafter. We did get it in the black, however.

The Ball family in the Olive Ann Beech Gallery — October, 1976.

THE BONANZA MODELS

H ere we will cover, with as much detail as possible, every model of the Bonanza as it was delivered from the Factory, since 1972, earlier models are covered in my previous book, *Those Incomparable Bonanzas*. Since the Bonanza has been the modification buff's dream project throughout the years, it is unlikely any of the early airplanes are still in the original factory configuration. Sooner or later almost every Bonanza falls into the hands of an aficionado who will try to make it as much like a new production unit as is humanly possible. It can't be done, of course, but many owners have come close to duplicating at least the external appearance of a fresh-off-the-line, current model. Beech has helped by making available numerous improvement kits when demand has warranted it.

Realizing the pitfalls then, we will describe every model as it rolled out the doors at Wichita, Kansas. Many of the changes that occurred during the production run of each model are also listed. Some of these changes are major, some very minor in nature. The small changes are included for three reasons. They may be of significance to some readers, they make the record more complete, and frankly it is sometimes difficult to draw a line between what is important and what is not.

Generally, unless otherwise noted, each succeeding model will include the features of the prior model. Performance data is repeated, however, even though it may not have changed from the previous model. This was done so it would not be necessary to refer back to an earlier model or models to obtain a complete set of numbers. Where performance has changed it is called to your attention in the text.

All performance figures are at full gross weight, standard day. A minor reduction in factory listed performance between models with the same engine is usually caused by an increase in gross weight. Where gross weight has increased with no reduction in performance (with the same engine) several explanations could apply. The decrease was hardly measurable, there was a small offsetting aerodynamic cleanup, or the average performance of production airplanes was better than originally anticipated.

Minor range variations occur between some models with the same engine, gross weight, and fuel capacity because of a difference in altitude and speed used by the factory to calculate maximum range, or a difference in what is considered to be usable fuel.

For their historical value we have included fly-away-factory base prices, including any price changes that occurred during the production run.

The information presented in this section of the book should not be used in lieu of the appropriate Bonanza owner's manual.

V35B

BONANZA

MODEL YEAR 1972

Top speed at sea level. . . . . 210 MPH
Maximum recommended cruise power . . . . 75% (214 HP)
Cruise speed at 75% power at 6500 feet (optimum altitude)
     full throttle, 2500 RPM. . . . . 203 MPH
Standard fuel capacity. . . . . 50 gallons
Maximum range (at 163 MPH at 10,000 feet)
     with standard tanks. . . . . 600 miles
     with extended range tanks (80 gallons total) . . . . 1110 miles
(Ranges include allowance for warm-up, taxi, takeoff, climb,
     and a 45-minute reserve at 45% power.)
Gross weight . . . . 3400 pounds
Empty weight (includes standard avionics) . . . . 1985 pounds
Useful load . . . . 1415 pounds

Stall speed (landing, full flaps) . . . . 63 MPH
Rate of climb at sea level . . . . 1136 feet per minute
Service ceiling . . . . 17,500 feet

Airspeed limits Maneuvering . . . . 152 MPH
                Maximum structural cruising. . . . . 190 MPH
                Never exceed. . . . . 225 MPH
                Flaps extended (normal) . . . . 140 MPH
                Landing gear extended (normal) . . . . 175 MPH
Fuel. . . . . 100/130 octane minimum

The model designation didn't change from the previous model, but nevertheless, the 1972 edition of the V35B is considered a model change. The interior underwent a major redesign which was so extensive that many structural changes had to be made in the cabin — particularly the roof — to accommodate the all new interior. The 1972 V35B Bonanza features a more durable interior with an improved overhead ventilation system and more head room. Cabin chairs and the instrument panel were also restyled. It can also be distinguished from earlier V35Bs by its new paint design. Power plant was the Continental IO-520-BA rated at 285 H.P. Empty weight is up slightly over that of the 1971 V35B, otherwise performance is unchanged.

Serials of 1972 V35B production start with D-9287. The price was initially $41,600, later increased to $46,000. The last 1972 V35B was D-9390, a total of 104 units.

THESE CHANGES OCCURRED DURING PRODUCTION:

- Beef-up E.L.T. mounting bracket, D-9386 and after,
- Improve radio shelf assembly, D-9350 and after,
- New E.L.T. antenna doubler, D-9370 and after,
- Edo-Aire Mitchell Century I Flight System, D-9356 and after.

V35B

BONANZA

MODEL YEAR 1973

Top speed at sea level . . . . 210 MPH
Maximum recommended cruise power . . . . 75% (214 HP)
Cruise speed at 75% power at 6500 feet (optimum altitude)
     full throttle, 2500 RPM . . . . 203 MPH
Standard fuel capacity . . . . 44 gallons
Maximum range (at 163 MPH at 10,000 feet)
     with standard tanks . . . . 530 miles
     with extended range tanks (74 gallons total) . . . . 891 miles
(Ranges include allowance for warm-up, taxi, takeoff, climb,
     and a 45-minute reserve at 45% power.)
Gross weight . . . . 3400 pounds
Empty weight (includes standard avionics) . . . . 1985 pounds
Useful load . . . . 1415 pounds

Stall speed (landing, full flaps) . . . . 63 MPH
Rate of climb at sea level . . . . 1136 feet per minute
Service ceiling . . . . 17,500 feet

Airspeed limits   Maneuvering . . . . 152 MPH
                  Maximum structural cruising . . . . 190 MPH
                  Never exceed . . . . 225 MPH
                  Flaps extended (normal) . . . . 140 MPH
                  Landing gear extended (normal) . . . . 175 MPH
Fuel . . . . 100/130 octane minimum

The 1973 V35B Bonanza had the same paint design as the 1972 model. Serial numbers start with D-9391 and run through D-9537, a total of 147 units. Power Plant was once again the Continental IO-520-BA rated at 285 H.P. Price was unchanged at $46,000.

THESE CHANGES OCCURRED DURING PRODUCTION:

- Eliminate vertical instruments by installing an Edo-Aire Wet Line Engine Cluster, D-9391 and after,

- Openable window latching system improvement, D-9412 and after,

- Additional seat track stops, D-9399 and after,

- Chemical film treatment — Exterior Skins, D-9503 and after,

- Improved air pump filter, D-9508 and after,

- Improved fuel tank sight gage, D-9421 and after,

- Relocation of main landing gear torque knee lubrication, D-9468 and after,

- Openable cabin window seal change, D-9484 and after,

- Gust lock improvement, D-9512 and after,

- Aft cowl door handle, D-9537 and after.

V35B
BONANZA

MODEL YEAR 1974

Top speed at sea level.................................... 210 MPH
Maximum recommended cruise power .... 75% (214 HP)
Cruise speed at 75% power at 6500 feet (optimum altitude)
    full throttle, 2500 RPM.............................. 203 MPH
Standard fuel capacity.................................... 44 gallons
Maximum range (at 163 MPH at 10,000 feet)
    with standard tanks................................... 530 miles
    with extended range tanks (74 gallons total) .... 900 miles
(Ranges include allowance for warm-up, taxi, takeoff, climb,
    and a 45-minute reserve at 45% power.)
Gross weight .... 3400 pounds
Empty weight (includes standard avionics) .... 2031 pounds
Useful load .... 1381 pounds

Stall speed (landing, full flaps) .... 63 MPH
Rate of climb at sea level .... 1136 feet per minute
Service ceiling .... 17,500 feet

Airspeed limits   Maneuvering .... 152 MPH
                  Maximum structural cruising............... 190 MPH
                  Never exceed........................... 225 MPH
                  Flaps extended (normal) .... 140 MPH
                  Landing gear extended (normal) .... 175 MPH
Fuel..................................... 100/130 octane minimum

The 1974 V35B Bonanza sported a new paint design and began with serial number D-9538 and ran through D-9686, a total of 149 units. Power Plant was the Continental IO-520-BA rated at 285 H.P. The 1974 price was $47,350.

THESE CHANGES OCCURRED DURING PRODUCTION:

- Utility baggage door frame (one piece inner and one piece outer) D-9641 and after,
- Engine cowl reinforcement, D-9559 and after,
- Heat and vent air flow improvement, D-9650 and after,
- Dual landing gear safety switch, D-9681 and after,
- Strobe light grounding improvement, D-9655 and after.

V35B

BONANZA

MODEL YEAR 1975

Top speed at sea level.................................... 210 MPH
Maximum recommended cruise power.................. 75% (214 HP)
Cruise speed at 75% power at 6500 feet (optimum altitude)
    full throttle, 2500 RPM............................... 203 MPH
Standard fuel capacity.................................... 44 gallons
Maximum range (at 163 MPH at 10,000 feet)
    with standard tanks.................................. 530 miles
    with extended range tanks (74 gallons total)............ 900 miles
(Ranges include allowance for warm-up, taxi, takeoff, climb,
    and a 45-minute reserve at 45% power.)
Gross weight .... 3400 pounds
Empty weight (includes standard avionics) .... 2051 pounds
Useful load .... 1361 pounds

Stall speed (landing, full flaps) .... 63 MPH
Rate of climb at sea level .... 1136 feet per minute
Service ceiling .... 17,500 feet

Airspeed limits   Maneuvering .... 152 MPH
               Maximum structural cruising............... 190 MPH
               Never exceed........................... 225 MPH
               Flaps extended (normal) .... 140 MPH
               Landing gear extended (normal) .... 175 MPH
Fuel.................................... 100/130 octane minimum

The paint design remained unchanged on the 1975 V35B Bonanza. Serial numbers began with D-9687 and ended with D-9815. A total of 129 units. The Power Plant was the Continental IO-520-BA rated at 285 H.P. The 1975 price was $55,400.

THESE CHANGES OCCURRED DURING PRODUCTION:

- Explosion containing strobe lights, D-9693 and after,
- Air conditioning installation, D-9787, D-9806 and after,
- IO-520-BA spec 12 engine with drive for air conditioning, D-9775 and after,
- Barry engine mounts, D-9767, D-9768 and D-9772,
- IO-520-BA spec 10 engine with Slick mags, D-9738 through D-9752 only,
- Electro Mech landing gear motor, D-9807 and after,
- Gust lock redesign, D-9705 and after,
- Barry engine mounts, D-9767, D-9768, D-9772 only,
- IO-520-BA spec 10 engine with Slick mags, D-9738 through D-9752 only.

V35B

BONANZA   **MODEL YEAR 1976**

Top speed at sea level.................................... 210 MPH
Maximum recommended cruise power .... 75% (214 HP)
Cruise speed at 75% power at 6500 feet (optimum altitude)
     full throttle, 2500 RPM................................ 203 MPH
Standard fuel capacity..................................... 44 gallons
Maximum range (at 163 MPH at 10,000 feet)
     with standard tanks.................................... 530 miles
     with extended range tanks (74 gallons total) .... 900 miles
(Ranges include allowance for warm-up, taxi, takeoff, climb,
     and a 45-minute reserve at 45% power.)
Gross weight .... 3400 pounds
Empty weight (includes standard avionics) .... 2051 pounds
Useful load .... 1361 pounds

Stall speed (landing, full flaps) .... 63 MPH
Rate of climb at sea level .... 1136 feet per minute
Service ceiling .... 17,500 feet

Airspeed limits Maneuvering .... 152 MPH
                Maximum structural cruising............... 190 MPH
                Never exceed........................... 225 MPH
                Flaps extended (normal) .... 140 MPH
                Landing gear extended (normal) .... 175 MPH
Fuel.................................... 100/130 octane minimum

The 1976 V35B Bonanza had a new interior but the same paint design as the 1975 V35B. Serial numbers began with D-9816 and ended with D-9947. For a total of 132 units. The engine was the IO-520-BA Continental rated at 285 H.P. The standard equipped price was $61,650.

THESE CHANGES OCCURRED DURING PRODUCTION:

- Bonded cowl door, D-9924 only,
- One piece cabin door frame for a better fit, D-9819, D-9856 and after,
- Pilot and passenger shoulder restraints, D-9862 and after.

V35B

BONANZA   **MODEL YEAR 1977**

Top speed at sea level. . . . . 209 MPH
Maximum recommended cruise power . . . . 75% (214 HP)
Cruise speed at 75% power at 6500 feet (optimum altitude)
      full throttle, 2500 RPM. . . . . 198 MPH
Standard fuel capacity. . . . . 44 gallons
Maximum range (at 163 MPH at 10,000 feet)
      with standard tanks. . . . . 530 miles
      with extended range tanks (74 gallons total) . . . . 894 miles
    (Ranges include allowance for warm-up, taxi, takeoff, climb,
        and a 45-minute reserve at 45% power.)
Gross weight . . . . 3400 pounds
Empty weight (includes standard avionics) . . . . 2087 pounds
Useful load . . . . 1325 pounds

Stall speed (landing, full flaps) . . . . 59 MPH
Rate of climb at sea level . . . . 1167 feet per minute
Service ceiling . . . . 17,858 feet

Airspeed limits   Maneuvering . . . . 152 MPH
                Maximum structural cruising. . . . . 190 MPH
                Never exceed. . . . . 225 MPH
                Flaps extended (normal) . . . . 140 MPH
                Landing gear extended (normal) . . . . 175 MPH
Fuel. . . . . 100/130 octane minimum

The 1977 V35B had a new paint design. Serial numbers began with D-9948 and ran through D-10068. For a total of 121 units. Power Plant was the Continental IO-520-BA rated at 285 H.P. The price was $65,950.

THESE CHANGES OCCURRED DURING PRODUCTION:

- Oxygen mask containers, D-9948 and after,
- Airspeed change — knots on the outside, D-9948 and after,
- Inertia reel installation — pilot and copilot, D-10016 and after,
- Deletion of sixth seat, D-9948 and after,
- 24 Volt electrical system, D-10097, D-10120 and after,
- Quartz digital chronometer, D-10024 and after,
- Standby generator functional test, D-10035 and after.

10,000th Beechcraft Bonanza 35 (V35B) — 1977.

Roll-out of 10,000th Beechcraft Bonanza Model 35, — February 9, 1977.

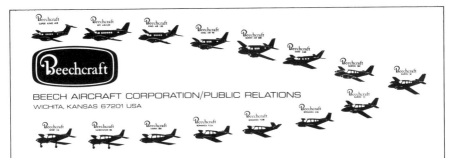

BEECH AIRCRAFT CORPORATION/PUBLIC RELATIONS
WICHITA, KANSAS 67201 USA

Beechcraft Bonanza D-10,000

Reflects 30 Years Of Refinements

Thirty years of production -- 10,000 Beechcraft Bonanzas -- "How do we express the way Beech Aircraft and its people feel about such a milestone by the way we finish one airplane?" This was the challenge before Beechcraft styling engineers in choosing appointments for the 10,000th Beechcraft Bonanza Model 35.

The company's experts suddenly found themselves on the other side of the desk, facing the same dilemma as any Beechcraft Bonanza customer and learned that choosing from the industry's widest selection of interior and exterior options is no simple task.

With silver and blue selected as the aircraft's predominant colors, the Beech stylists set about doing what they have been helping customers do for 30 years, obtaining coordinated paints, fabrics and leathers from some of the world's most exclusive suppliers.

Regal blue and silver frost metallic urethane paints add a deep glow to the exterior. Specially-cast 'Bonanza D-10,000' emblems on the cowls further emphasize the uniqueness of N35VB.

On the inside, the silver seats are made of leather from the same company in Scotland which supplies leathers for Rolls Royce automobiles. Matching seat inserts are mohair crushed velvet imported from the Netherlands and the plush blue carpet is the last of a limited edition.

-more-

889-36067

State-of-the-art avionics from Collins, Edo-Aire Mitchell and Narco, coupled with Beech Aircraft's latest features for flight safety and passenger comfort, make this Beechcraft Bonanza V35B, as all the other Bonanzas before it, a leader in quality, performance and luxury among the world's single-engine aircraft.

-315-

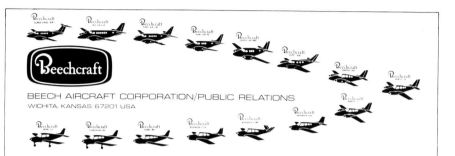

Beechcraft

BEECH AIRCRAFT CORPORATION/PUBLIC RELATIONS
WICHITA, KANSAS 67201 USA

10,000th Beechcraft Bonanza Model 35

Now On Nationwide Tour

On February 17, 1977, the 10,000th Beechcraft Bonanza Model 35 was released from production flight tests -- exactly 30 years and two days after the first Bonanza Model 35 was delivered on February 15, 1947.

While it looks similar to other current Beechcraft Bonanza V35B production models, except for its own special paint and customized interior, the significance of serial number D-10,000 is that this classic V-tail design has been in continuous production for over 30 years.

Today's Beechcraft Bonanza 35 has much the same external appearance as did the first model, but through the years has been continually refined to reflect the latest technology with addition of more horsepower, larger cabin windows, sparkling paint designs, luxurious interior appointments and sophisticated avionics. But it retains the same basic design that has held the loyalty and admiration of its owners and pilots for over three decades.

Production of Beechcraft Bonanza D-10,000 began on December 27, 1976 when work on its wings was started at Beechcraft's Salina, Kansas Division. Control surfaces were completed on January 13, 1977 at the Liberal, Kansas Division, while its spar center section was being completed at the Boulder, Colorado Division.

Final assembly was performed in Wichita. Painting was completed on January 27

-more-

and Model 35 D-10,000 rolled off the assembly line on February 9, ready for flight tests and the stamp of acceptance.

Following introduction to aviation press representatives in early March, the 10,000th Beechcraft Bonanza Model 35 will be on display around the United States through September of this year.

Beechcraft Aviation Centers will display Bonanza D-10,000 at special open house occasions, and the famous milestone aircraft will be featured at such national aviation events as Reading Air Show, Flying Dentists' and Flying Physicians' annual conventions, the Experimental Aircraft Association's Convention and Exhibition, and the American Bonanza Society Convention in Milwaukee, Wisconsin.

The final display of Bonanza D-10,000 will be in Wichita when the aircraft returns for the Beechcraft International Sales Conference next fall.

-315-

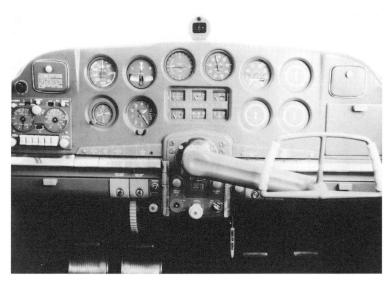

1947 Beechcraft Bonanza 35 panel.

1977 Beechcraft Bonanza V35B panel.

V35B

BONANZA

MODEL YEAR 1978

Top speed at sea level.................................... 209 MPH
Maximum recommended cruise power .... 75% (214 HP)
Cruise speed at 75% power at 6500 feet (optimum altitude)
    full throttle, 2500 RPM............................... 198 MPH
Standard fuel capacity..................................... 44 gallons
Maximum range (at 163 MPH at 10,000 feet)
    with standard tanks.................................... 530 miles
    with extended range tanks (74 gallons total) .... 894 miles
(Ranges include allowance for warm-up, taxi, takeoff, climb,
    and a 45-minute reserve at 45% power.)
Gross weight .... 3400 pounds
Empty weight (includes standard avionics) .... 2093 pounds
Useful load .... 1394 pounds

Stall speed (landing, full flaps) .... 59 MPH
Rate of climb at sea level .... 1167 feet per minute
Service ceiling .... 17,858 feet

Airspeed limits   Maneuvering .... 152 MPH
                Maximum structural cruising............... 190 MPH
                Never exceed........................... 225 MPH
                Flaps extended (normal) .... 140 MPH
                Landing gear extended (normal) .... 175 MPH
Fuel.................................... 100/130 octane minimum

The 1978 V35B Bonanza had a new interior but the same exterior paint design as the 1977 model. Serial numbers began with D-10069 and ended with D-10178. A total of 110 units. Power was provided by the Continental IO-520-BA rated at 285 H.P. The standard equipped price was $72,575.

THESE CHANGES OCCURRED DURING PRODUCTION:

- New seals for openable windows, D-10091, D-10099, D-10101 and after,
- Torque adjusting sunvisors, D-10172 and after,
- 28-volt propeller de-ice, D-10144 and after.

V35B

BONANZA

Top speed at sea level . . . . 209 MPH
Maximum recommended cruise power . . . . 75% (214 HP)
Cruise speed at 75% power at 6000 feet (optimum altitude)
    full throttle, 2500 RPM . . . . 198 MPH
Standard fuel capacity . . . . 44 gallons
Maximum range (at 163 MPH at 10,000 feet)
    with standard tanks . . . . 530 miles
    with extended range tanks (74 gallons total) . . . . 894 miles
(Ranges include allowance for warm-up, taxi, takeoff, climb,
      and a 45-minute reserve at 45% power.)
Gross weight . . . . 3400 pounds
Empty weight (includes standard avionics) . . . . 2094 pounds
Useful load . . . . 1318 pounds

Stall speed (landing, full flaps) . . . . 59 MPH
Rate of climb at sea level . . . . 1167 feet per minute
Service ceiling . . . . 17,858 feet

Airspeed limits   Maneuvering . . . . 152 MPH
                     Maximum structural cruising . . . . 190 MPH
                     Never exceed . . . . 225 MPH
                     Flaps extended (normal) . . . . 140 MPH
                     Landing gear extended (normal) . . . . 175 MPH
Fuel . . . . 100/130 octane minimum

The 1979 V35B had a new interior but the same exterior paint design as the 1977 and 1978 models. Serial numbers begin with D-10179 and end with D-10302 . . . 124 units. Power was the new Continental IO-520-BB rated at 285 H.P. The standard equipped price was $82,150.

THESE CHANGES OCCURRED DURING PRODUCTION:

- Aft cabin exhaust air drain added, D-10200 and after,
- Flap switch has approach position added, D-10179 and after,
- Standby generator — 28 volts, D-10206 and after,
- TCM 100 AMP alternator, D-10248 and after,
- Series plumbing for dual brakes, D-10213 and after,
- Floating panel bonding strap, D-10239 and after,
- Nose gear rod retract boot, D-10269 and after,
- Radar antenna installation, leading edge, right wing, D-10264 and after,
- Liquid crystal digital clock, D-10248 and after.

V35B

BONANZA

Top speed at sea level. . . . . 209 MPH
Maximum recommended cruise power . . . . 75% (214 HP)
Cruise speed at 75% power at 6000 feet (optimum altitude)
    full throttle, 2500 RPM. . . . . 198 MPH
Standard fuel capacity. . . . . 74 gallons
Maximum range (at 163 MPH at 10,000 feet)
    with standard tanks. . . . . 894 miles
(Range includes allowance for warm-up, taxi, takeoff, climb,and a 45-minute
    reserve at 45% power.)
Gross weight . . . . 3400 pounds
Empty weight (includes standard avionics) . . . . 2117 pounds
Useful load . . . . 1295 pounds

Stall speed (landing, full flaps) . . . . 59 MPH
Rate of climb at sea level . . . . 1167 feet per minute
Service ceiling . . . . 17,858 feet

Airspeed limits   Maneuvering . . . . 152 MPH
                  Maximum structural cruising. . . . . 190 MPH
                  Never exceed. . . . . 225 MPH
                  Flaps extended (normal) . . . . 140 MPH
                  Landing gear extended (normal) . . . . 175 MPH
Fuel. . . . . 100/130 octane minimum

The 1980 V35B had a new paint design and new interior. Serial numbers began with D-10303 and ended with D-10353 . . . 51 units. Power was the Continental IO-520-BB rated at 285 H.P. The standard equipped price was $91,950.

THESE CHANGES OCCURRED DURING PRODUCTION:

- New voltage regulator, D-10332 and after,
- New improved landing gear motor, D-10325 and after,
- Airspeed indicator with approach flap white triangle, D-10303 and after,
- 80 Gallon fuel system as standard fuel, D-10303 and after,
- External power relay control, D-10319 and after,
- 1980 External noise level reduction, D-10313 and after,
- Openable window latch improvement, D-10348, D-10353 and after,
- Knots only airspeed standard D-10348,
- Openable window latch revision, D-10353 and after,
- Hartzell propeller standard, D-10350 and after,
- Engine fuel system adjustment procedure, D-10351 and after,
- Fresh air cabin blower, D-10348.

V35B

BONANZA

MODEL YEAR 1981

Top speed at sea level.................................... 209 MPH
Maximum recommended cruise power.................. 75% (214 HP)
Cruise speed at 75% power at 6000 feet (optimum altitude)
    full throttle, 2500 RPM.............................. 193 MPH
Standard fuel capacity.................................... 74 gallons
Maximum range (at 163 MPH at 10,000 feet)
    with standard tanks................................. 894 miles
(Range includes allowance for warm-up, taxi, takeoff, climb, and a 45-minute
    reserve at 45% power.)
Gross weight .... 3400 pounds
Empty weight (includes standard avionics) .... 2106 pounds
Useful load .... 1306 pounds

Stall speed (landing, full flaps) .... 59 MPH
Rate of climb at sea level .... 1167 feet per minute
Service ceiling .... 17,858 feet

Airspeed limits Maneuvering .... 152 MPH
                Maximum structural cruising............... 190 MPH
                Never exceed........................... 225 MPH
                Flaps extended (normal) .... 140 MPH
                Landing gear extended (normal) .... 175 MPH
Fuel.................................... 100/130 octane minimum

The 1981 V35B Bonanza had no interior or exterior changes from the 1980 model. Serial numbers began with D-10354 and ended with D-10382... 29 units. Power was the Continental IO-520-BB rated at 285 H.P. The standard equipped price was $108,000.

THESE CHANGES OCCURRED DURING PRODUCTION:

- Improved dynamic brake relay, D-10379 and after,
- Reduced aileron free play, D-10376 and after,
- 60 AMP Teledyne Crittenden alternator, D-10354 and after,
- Longer control column to protect radios, D-10359 and after,
- Knots only airspeed indicator, D-10354 and after,
- Fresh air blower, D-10364 and after,
- Change in engine winter baffles, D-10354 and after.

V35B

BONANZA

Top speed at sea level.................................... 209 MPH

Maximum recommended cruise power .... 75% (214 HP)

Cruise speed at 75% power at 6000 feet (optimum altitude)
  full throttle, 2500 RPM............................... 198 MPH

Standard fuel capacity.................................... 74 Gallons

Maximum range (at 163 MPH at 10,000 feet)
  with standard tanks.................................. 894 miles
  (Range includes allowance for warm-up, taxi, takeoff, climb, and a 45-minute
    reserve at 45% power.)

Gross weight .... 3400 pounds

Empty weight (includes standard avionics) .... 2110 pounds

Useful load .... 1302 pounds

Stall speed (landing, full flaps) ....59 MPH

Rate of climb at sea level .... 1167 feet per minute

Service ceiling ....17,858 feet

Airspeed limits Maneuvering .... 152 MPH

                 Maximum structural cruising............... 190 MPH

                 Never exceed........................... 225 MPH

                 Flaps extended (normal) .... 140 MPH

                 Landing gear extended (normal) .... 175 MPH

Fuel.................................... 100/130 octane minimum

The 1982 V35B Bonanza was the last of the V-Tails. There were no interior or exterior changes from the 1981 model. Serial numbers began with D-10383 and ended with D-10403 . . . only 21 units. Power was the Continental IO-520-BB rated at 285 H.P. The standard equipped price was $118,750.

THESE CHANGES OCCURRED DURING PRODUCTION:

- New static wick installation, D-10383 and after,
- Change in openable window latch mechanism, D-10386 and after,
- Aircraft corrosion proofing becomes standard, D-10383 and after,
- Propeller de-ice installation, D-10400 and after,
- Improved alternator voltage regulator, D-10392 and after,
- Improved TCM compressor drive kit, D-10395 and after,
- Instrument panel laminate, woodgrain, D-10403 only.

PUBLIC RELATIONS
BEECH AIRCRAFT CORPORATION
WICHITA, KANSAS 67201 USA

March, 1982

35TH ANNIVERSARY BEECHCRAFT BONANZA ROLLED OUT;

BEGINS NATIONWIDE TOUR

WICHITA, KAN. -- In ceremonies March 25 at its Wichita headquarters, Beech Aircraft Corporation, a subsidiary of Raytheon Company, rolled out a specially-appointed 35th anniversary edition of the Beechcraft Bonanza Model V35B.

The airplane commemorates 35 years' production of the popular V-tail high performance, single-engine business aircraft.

Following the ceremonies, the airplane began a coast-to-coast tour of Beechcraft franchises and aviation events, celebrating the 50th Anniversary of Beech Aircraft Corporation and the 35th Anniversary of the Beechcraft Bonanza.

The Beechcraft Bonanza Model 35 was first certified on March 25, 1947. In the 35 years since, almost 15,000 Bonanzas, including almost 10,400 V-tail Model 35s, have been built.

In remarks during the rollout ceremony, Beech Aircraft Corporation President E.C. Burns praised the Beechcraft Bonanza, saying, "It has proved itself to be a reliable and economical airplane for business, for utility operation and personal flying.

"Among the world's lineup of single-engine airplanes, the Bonanza is still viewed as the pinnacle of ownership in the single-engine field."

President Burns was followed by American Bonanza Society President Tex Anderson, who said, "There are two kinds of pilots: those who own Bonanzas, and those who want to."

-more-

A Raytheon Company

889-36067

The Beechcraft Bonanza Model V35B is a four place, single-engine, high performance business and pleasure aircraft, licensed in utility category at maximum take-off weight. The Anniversary version is powered by a six-cylinder Continental IO-520-BB fuel-injected engine, rated at 285 hp., with an optional three-bladed, anti-icing propeller. A full IFR avionics package, along with a three-axis autopilot and flight director, is also installed in the aircraft.

The "35th Anniversary Bonanza" also features a one-time-only exterior paint design. Done in analogous shades of blue stripes over a Graystone base which highlights the distinctive V-tail, with a special "Thirty-Fifth Anniversary Bonanza" inscription painted on each wingtip, and with a custom designed leather interior to match, the airplane carries a suggested selling price of $216,672. Base price is $118,750.

-bac-

Contact: John Gedraitis
           (316) 681-7693

Beechcraft Bonanza 35, 1947.

35th Anniversary Beechcraft Bonanza.

F33A

BONANZA   **MODEL YEAR 1972**

Top speed at sea level.................................... 208 MPH
Maximum recommended cruise power .... 75% (214 HP)
Cruise speed at 75% power at 6500 feet (optimum altitude)
     full throttle, 2500 RPM.............................. 200 MPH
Standard fuel capacity.................................... 50 gallons
Maximum range (at 156 MPH at 10,000 feet)
     with standard tanks.................................. 595 miles
     with extended range tanks (80 gallons total) .... 1080 miles
(Ranges include allowance for warm-up, taxi, takeoff, climb,
     and a 45-minute reserve at 45% power.)
Gross weight .... 3400 pounds
Empty weight (includes standard avionics) .... 2000 pounds
Useful load .... 1400 pounds

Stall speed (landing, full flaps) ....63 MPH
Rate of climb at sea level .... 1136 feet per minute
Service ceiling .... 17,500 feet

Airspeed limits   Maneuvering .... 152 MPH
                     Maximum structural cruising............... 190 MPH
                     Never exceed........................... 225 MPH
                     Flaps extended (normal) .... 140 MPH
                     Landing gear extended (normal) .... 175 MPH
Fuel .... 100/130 octane minimum

Power Plant for the 1972 F33A was the Continental IO-520-BA rated at 285 HP.

No change in model designation from its 1971 counterpart, but the 1972 F33A did experience significant change. The interior underwent a major redesign which was so extensive many structural changes had to be made in the cabin, particularly the roof, to accommodate the all-new interior. This model features a more durable interior with more head room and an improved overhead ventilation system. Cabin chairs and the instrument panel were also restyled. Another significant development is the change to the all electric vertical readout engine instruments previously introduced on the 1971 V35B. The 1972 F33A has a new paint design to identify it from earlier models. Empty weight is up over that of the 1971 F33A, otherwise performance is unchanged.

Serials of the 1972 F33A production start with CE-350. The price was initially $41,600, later increased to $46,000. The last 1972 F33A was CE-401, a total of 52 units.

THESE CHANGES OCCURRED DURING PRODUCTION:

- Parking brake cable rerouted, CE-364 and after,
- Uplock roller grease bolt, main landing gear, CE-350 and after,
- Grimes three light strobe system, CE-371 and after,
- Standby generator, CE-374 and after,
- Shoulder harness — pilot and copilot, CE-358 and after,
- Emergency locator transmitter, CE-361 and after,
- Improved fuel quantity sensor, CE-354 and after,
- One piece nose bug, CE-390 and after,
- Increase unusable fuel, CE-367 and after,
- Bendix Model S6RN-1225 magnetos, CE-386 and after,
- Control column drive change, CE-394 and after,
- ELT bracket change, CE-399 and after,
- New ELT antenna doubler, CE-388 and after,
- Improved exhaust pipe support shock mounts, CE-392 and after,
- Landing gear safety system pressure switch, CE-401 and after,
- Start relay circuit breaker, CE-392 and after,
- Elevator horn change, CE-399 and after.

F33A

BONANZA

Top speed at sea level . . . . 208 MPH
Maximum recommended cruise power . . . . 75% (214 HP)
Cruise speed at 75% power at 6500 feet (optimum altitude)
    full throttle, 2500 RPM . . . . 200 MPH
Standard fuel capacity . . . . 44 gallons
Maximum range (at 156 MPH at 10,000 feet)
    with standard tanks . . . . 585 miles
    with extended range tanks (74 gallons total) . . . . 895 miles
(Ranges include allowance for warm-up, taxi, takeoff, climb,
    and a 45-minute reserve at 45% power.)
Gross weight . . . . 3400 pounds
Empty weight (includes standard avionics) . . . . 2000 pounds
Useful load . . . . 1400 pounds

Stall speed (landing, full flaps) . . . . 63 MPH
Rate of climb at sea level . . . . 1136 feet per minute
Service ceiling . . . . 17,500 feet

Airspeed limits   Maneuvering . . . . 152 MPH
                   Maximum structural cruising . . . . 190 MPH
                   Never exceed . . . . 225 MPH
                   Flaps extended (normal) . . . . 140 MPH
                   Landing gear extended (normal) . . . . 175 MPH
Fuel . . . . 100/130 octane minimum

No change in paint or interior for the 1973 F33A Bonanza. Serial numbers began with CE-402 and ended with CE-464 . . . a total of 63 units. The Power Plant was the Continental IO-520-BA rated at 285 H.P. The 1973 price was $46,000.

THESE CHANGES OCCURRED DURING PRODUCTION:

- Openable window latching system improvement, CE-416 and after,
- Additional seat track stops CE-404 and after,
- Chemical film treatment — exterior skins, CE-451 and after,
- Improved sight gage installation, CE-414 and after,
- Relocation of main landing gear torque knee lubricator, CE-435 and after,
- Openable window seal improvement, CE-426 and after,
- Gust lock improvement, CE-454 and after,
- Hanlon-Wilson 701-20 muffler and 701-21 heater, CE-471 and after,
- Aft cowl door handle, CE-464 and after,
- Change to light twin engine floating panel attach brackets, CE-412 and after,
- Vertical instruments replaced by Edo-Aire wet line cluster, Ce-409 and after.

F33A

BONANZA

Top speed at sea level. . . . . 208 MPH

Maximum recommended cruise power . . . . 75% (214 HP)

Cruise speed at 75% power at 6500 feet (optimum altitude)
      full throttle, 2500 RPM. . . . . 200 MPH

Standard fuel capacity. . . . . 44 gallons

Maximum range (at 156 MPH at 10,000 feet)
      with standard tanks. . . . . 585 miles
      with extended range tanks (74 gallons total) . . . . 895 miles

(Ranges include allowance for warm-up, taxi, takeoff, climb,
      and a 45-minute reserve at 45% power.)

Gross weight . . . . 3400 pounds

Empty weight (includes standard avionics) . . . . 2056 pounds

Useful load . . . . 1356 pounds

Stall speed (landing, full flaps) . . . . 63 MPH

Rate of climb at sea level . . . . 1136 feet per minute

Service ceiling . . . . 17,500 feet

Airspeed limits   Maneuvering . . . . 152 MPH
                     Maximum structural cruising. . . . . 190 MPH
                     Never exceed. . . . . 225 MPH
                     Flaps extended (normal) . . . . 140 MPH
                     Landing gear extended (normal) . . . . 175 MPH

Fuel . . . . 100/130 octane minimum

A changed paint design for the 1974 F33A Bonanza. The interior remained unchanged. Serial numbers began with CE-465 and ended with CE-535 . . . a total of 71 units. The Power Plant was the Continental IO-520-BA rated at 285 H.P. The 1974 price was $47,350.

THESE CHANGES OCCURRED DURING PRODUCTION:

- Engine cowl reinforcement, CE-475 and after,
- Heat and vent air flow improvement, CE-517 and after,
- Strobe light grounding improvement, CE-521 and after,
- Rudder and aileron control cable interconnect clearance improvement, CE-535 and after,
- One piece optional utility door frame for better fit, CE-511 and after.

F33A

BONANZA

Top speed at sea level. . . . . 208 MPH
Maximum recommended cruise power . . . . 75% (214 HP)
Cruise speed at 75% power at 6500 feet (optimum altitude)
    full throttle, 2500 RPM. . . . . 200 MPH
Standard fuel capacity. . . . . 44 gallons
Maximum range (at 156 MPH at 10,000 feet)
    with standard tanks. . . . . 585 miles
    with extended range tanks (74 gallons total) . . . . 895 miles
(Ranges include allowance for warm-up, taxi, takeoff, climb,
    and a 45-minute reserve at 45% power.)
Gross weight . . . . 3400 pounds
Empty weight (includes standard avionics) . . . . 2076 pounds
Useful load . . . . 1336 pounds

Stall speed (landing, full flaps) . . . . 63 MPH
Rate of climb at sea level . . . . 1136 feet per minute
Service ceiling . . . . 17,500 feet

Airspeed limits   Maneuvering . . . . 152 MPH
                Maximum structural cruising. . . . . 190 MPH
                Never exceed. . . . . 225 MPH
                Flaps extended (normal) . . . . 140 MPH
                Landing gear extended (normal) . . . . 175 MPH
Fuel. . . . . 100/130 octane minimum

The 1975 F33A Bonanza had the same interior and exterior paint design as the 1974 F33A. Serial numbers began with CE-536 and ended with CE-611 . . . a total of 76 units. The Power Plant was the Continental IO-520-BA rated at 285 H.P. The 1975 price was $55,400.

THESE CHANGES OCCURRED DURING PRODUCTION:

- Dual landing gear safety switch installation, CE-538 through CE-541, CE-543, CE-545, CE-546, CE-548, and after,
- Gust lock redesign, CE-545 and after except CE-547,
- Static wick material change, CE-578 and after,
- Explosion containing strobe light CE-581 and after,
- Provisions for air conditioning installation, CE-581 and after,
- Air conditioner installation, CE-602 and after,
- Floorboard change and parking brake relocation, CE-602 and after,
- Barry engine mounts, CE-577, CE-578, CE-580 only,
- IO-520-BA spec IO engine with Slick mags (662), CE-561 through CE-570 only.

F33A

BONANZA

Top speed at sea level . . . . 208 MPH
Maximum recommended cruise power . . . . 75% (214 HP)
Cruise speed at 75% power at 6500 feet (optimum altitude)
      full throttle, 2500 RPM . . . . 200 MPH
Standard fuel capacity . . . . 44 gallons
Maximum range (at 156 MPH at 10,000 feet)
      with standard tanks . . . . 585 miles
      with extended range tanks (74 gallons total) . . . . 895 miles
(Ranges include allowance for warm-up, taxi, takeoff, climb,
      and a 45-minute reserve at 45% power.)
Gross weight . . . . 3400 pounds
Empty weight (includes standard avionics) . . . . 2076 pounds
Useful load . . . . 1336 pounds

Stall speed (landing, full flaps) . . . . 63 MPH
Rate of climb at sea level . . . . 1136 feet per minute
Service ceiling . . . . 17,500 feet

Airspeed limits   Maneuvering . . . . 152 MPH
                 Maximum structural cruising . . . . 190 MPH
                 Never exceed . . . . 225 MPH
                 Flaps extended (normal) . . . . 140 MPH
                 Landing gear extended (normal) . . . . 175 MPH
Fuel . . . . 100/130 octane minimum

The 1976 F33A Bonanza had the same exterior paint design as the 1975 F33A, but did have a new interior. Serial numbers began with CE-612 and ended with CE-673...a total of 62 units. The Power Plant was the Continental IO-520-BA rated at 285 H.P. The 1976 price was $61,650.

THESE CHANGES OCCURRED DURING PRODUCTION:

- Pilot and passenger shoulder restraints, CE-634 and after,
- Bonded cowl door, CE-660 only. This cowling door could not be "beat and bash to fit",
- One piece cabin door frame for better fit, CE-633 and after.

F33A

BONANZA

MODEL YEAR 1977

Top speed at sea level . . . . 209 MPH
Maximum recommended cruise power . . . . 75% (214 HP)
Cruise speed at 75% power at 6000 feet (optimum altitude)
     full throttle, 2500 RPM . . . . 198 MPH
Standard fuel capacity . . . . 44 gallons
Maximum range (at 156 MPH at 10,000 feet)
     with standard tanks . . . . 585 miles
     with extended range tanks (74 gallons total) . . . . 894 miles
(Ranges include allowance for warm-up, taxi, takeoff, climb,
     and a 45-minute reserve at 45% power.)
Gross weight . . . . 3400 pounds
Empty weight (includes standard avionics) . . . . 2112 pounds
Useful load . . . . 1300 pounds

Stall speed (landing, full flaps) . . . . 59 MPH
Rate of climb at sea level . . . . 1167 feet per minute
Service ceiling . . . . 17,858 feet

Airspeed limits   Maneuvering . . . . 152 MPH
                  Maximum structural cruising . . . . 190 MPH
                  Never exceed . . . . 225 MPH
                  Flaps extended (normal) . . . . 140 MPH
                  Landing gear extended (normal) . . . . 175 MPH
Fuel . . . . 100/130 octane minimum

The 1977 F33A Bonanza had a new exterior paint design but an unchanged interior. Serial numbers began with CE-674 and ended with CE-743 . . . a total of 70 units. The Power Plant was the Continental IO-520-BA rated at 285 H.P. The 1977 price was $65,950.

THESE CHANGES OCCURRED DURING PRODUCTION:

- Oxygen mask containers are provided, CE-674 and after,
- Airspeed change — knots on the outside, CE-674 and after,
- Inertia reel installation — pilot and copilot, CE-712 and after,
- Dual brake plumbing routing change, CE-710 and after,
- Deletion of sixth seat for 1977, CE-674 and after,
- Quartz digital chronometer, CE-718 and after,
- Corrosion preventative treatment, elevator control push rods, CE-740 and after,
- Standby generator functional test, CE-725 and after,
- New seal for openable windows, CE-726 and after,
- Improved pilot and copilot seat frame, CE-678 and after,
- Shoulder harness inertial reels, CE-678 and after.

F33A
BONANZA

MODEL YEAR 1978

Top speed at sea level . . . . 209 MPH
Maximum recommended cruise power . . . . 75% (214 HP)
Cruise speed at 75% power at 6000 feet (optimum altitude)
    full throttle, 2500 RPM . . . . 198 MPH
Standard fuel capacity . . . . 44 gallons
Maximum range (at 156 MPH at 10,000 feet)
    with standard tanks . . . . 585 miles
    with extended range tanks (74 gallons total) . . . . 894 miles
(Ranges include allowance for warm-up, taxi, takeoff, climb,
    and a 45-minute reserve at 45% power.)
Gross weight . . . . 3400 pounds
Empty weight (includes standard avionics) . . . . 2107 pounds
Useful load . . . . 1305 pounds

Stall speed (landing, full flaps) . . . . 59 MPH
Rate of climb at sea level . . . . 1167 feet per minute
Service ceiling . . . . 17,858 feet

Airspeed limits   Maneuvering . . . . 152 MPH
                      Maximum structural cruising . . . . 190 MPH
                      Never exceed . . . . 225 MPH
                      Flaps extended (normal) . . . . 140 MPH
                      Landing gear extended (normal) . . . . 175 MPH
Fuel . . . . 100/130 octane minimum

122

The 1979 F33A Bonanza had the same interior and exterior paint design as the 1978 F33A. Serial numbers began with CE-816 and ended with CE-883 . . . a total of 68 units. The Power Plant was the new Continental IO-520-BB rated at 285 H.P. The 1979 price was $82,150.

THESE CHANGES OCCURRED DURING PRODUCTION:

- Duct installation — cabin air exhaust drain, CE-831 and after,
- Approach flap position on flap control, CE-816 and after,
- Standby generator — 28 volt CE-834 and after,
- TCM 100 AMP alternator, CE-862 and after,
- Series plumbing for dual brakes, CE-839 and after,
- Floating panel bonding strap, CE-857 and after,
- Liquid crystal digital clock, CE-862 and after,
- Radar antenna installation, CE-878 and after,
- Improved openable window seals, CE-844 and after.

F33A

BONANZA

Top speed at sea level . . . . 209 MPH
Maximum recommended cruise power . . . . 75% (214 HP)
Cruise speed at 75% power at 6000 feet (optimum altitude)
    full throttle, 2500 RPM . . . . 198 MPH
Standard fuel capacity . . . . 74 gallons
Maximum range (at 156 MPH at 10,000 feet)
    with standard tanks . . . . 894 miles
(Range includes allowance for warm-up, taxi, takeoff, climb,
    and a 45-minute reserve at 45% power.)
Gross weight . . . . 3400 pounds
Empty weight (includes standard avionics) . . . . 2132 pounds
Useful load . . . . 1280 pounds

Stall speed (landing, full flaps) . . . . 59 MPH
Rate of climb at sea level . . . . 1167 feet per minute
Service ceiling . . . . 17,858 feet

Airspeed limits   Maneuvering . . . . 152 MPH
                     Maximum structural cruising . . . . 190 MPH
                     Never exceed . . . . 225 MPH
                     Flaps extended (normal) . . . . 140 MPH
                     Landing gear extended (normal) . . . . 175 MPH
Fuel . . . . 100/130 octane minimum

The 1980 F33A Bonanza sported a new paint design. Serial numbers began with CE-884 and ended with CE-928 . . . a total of 45 units. The power plant was the Continental IO-520-BB rated at 285 H.P. The 1980 price $91,950.

THESE CHANGES OCCURRED DURING PRODUCTION:

- Reduced aileron freeplay, CE-914 and after,
- New voltage regulator, CE-898 and after,
- Airspeed indicator with approach flap white triangle, CE-884 and after,
- External power relay control, CE-892 and after,
- 1980 noise level reduction, CE-891 and after,
- 80 gallon fuel system standard CE-884 and after,
- Openable window latch improvement, CE-919, CE-923, CE-925, CE-927,
- Improved liquid crystal digital clock, CE-887 and after,
- Longer control column assembly to protect radios, CE-913 and after,
- Turn coordinator with power indication, lighted, CE-902 and after; unlighted, CE-904 and after,
- Openable window latch revision, CE-927 and after,
- Narco ELT installation, CE-906 and after.
- 60 AMP Teledyne Crittenden alternator, CE-926 and after.

F33A

BONANZA

Top speed at sea level. . . . . 209 MPH
Maximum recommended cruise power . . . . 75% (214 HP)
Cruise speed at 75% power at 6000 feet (optimum altitude)
    full throttle, 2500 RPM. . . . . 198 MPH
Standard fuel capacity. . . . . 74 gallons
Maximum range (at 156 MPH at 10,000 feet)
    with standard tanks. . . . . 894 miles
(Range includes allowance for warm-up, taxi, takeoff, climb,
      and a 45-minute reserve at 45% power.)
Gross weight . . . . 3400 pounds
Empty weight (includes standard avionics) . . . . 2125 pounds
Useful load . . . . 1287 pounds

Stall speed (landing, full flaps) . . . . 59 MPH
Rate of climb at sea level . . . . 1167 feet per minute
Service ceiling . . . . 17,858 feet

Airspeed limits   Maneuvering . . . . 152 MPH
                      Maximum structural cruising. . . . . 190 MPH
                      Never exceed. . . . . 225 MPH
                      Flaps extended (normal) . . . . 140 MPH
                      Landing gear extended (normal) . . . . 175 MPH
Fuel. . . . . 100/130 octane minimum

The 1981 F33A Bonanza had the same paint design as the 1980 F33A. Serial numbers began with CE-929 and ended with CE-977 . . . a total of 49 units. The Power Plant was the Continental IO-520-BB rated at 285 H.P. The 1981 price was $108,000.

THESE CHANGES OCCURRED DURING PRODUCTION:

- Aerosonic fuel flow system, CE-929 and after,
- Cabin fresh air blower, CE-941 and after,
- New engine winter baffles, CE-929 and after,
- Improved dynamic brake relay, CE-968 and after,

F33A

BONANZA

MODEL YEAR 1982

Top speed at sea level . . . . 209 MPH
Maximum recommended cruise power . . . . 75% (214 HP)
Cruise speed at 75% power at 6000 feet (optimum altitude)
    full throttle, 2500 RPM . . . . 198 MPH
Standard fuel capacity . . . . 74 gallons
Maximum range (at 156 MPH at 10,000 feet)
    with standard tanks . . . . 894 miles
(Range includes allowance for warm-up, taxi, takeoff, climb,
    and a 45-minute reserve at 45% power.)
Gross weight . . . . 3400 pounds
Empty weight (includes standard avionics) . . . . 2125 pounds
Useful load . . . . 1287 pounds

Stall speed (landing, full flaps) . . . . 59 MPH
Rate of climb at sea level . . . . 1167 feet per minute
Service ceiling . . . . 17,858 feet

Airspeed limits   Maneuvering . . . . 152 MPH
                 Maximum structural cruising . . . . 190 MPH
                 Never exceed . . . . 225 MPH
                 Flaps extended (normal) . . . . 140 MPH
                 Landing gear extended (normal) . . . . 175 MPH
Fuel . . . . 100/130 octane minimum

No change in exterior paint design or interior for the 1982 F33A Bonanza. Serial numbers began with CE-978 and ended with CE-1011 ... a total of 34 units. The Power Plant was the Continental IO-520-BB rated at 285 H.P. The 1982 standard equipped price was $118,750.

THESE CHANGES OCCURRED DURING PRODUCTION:

- New static wick installation, CE-978 and after,
- New openable window latch mechanism, CE-984 and after,
- Standard aircraft corrosion proofing, CE-978 and after,
- Optional propeller de-ice installation available, CE-1006 and after,
- Improved alternator voltage regulator, CE-994 and after,
- Improved TCM compressor drive kit, CE-999 and after.

F33A

BONANZA
MODEL YEAR 1983

Top speed at sea level.................................... 209 MPH
Maximum recommended cruise power.................. 75% (214 HP)
Cruise speed at 75% power at 6000 feet (optimum altitude)
    full throttle, 2500 RPM............................... 198 MPH
Standard fuel capacity...................................... 74 gallons
Maximum range (at 156 MPH at 10,000 feet)
    with standard tanks................................... 894 miles
(Range includes allowance for warm-up, taxi, takeoff, climb,
    and a 45-minute reserve at 45% power.)
Gross weight .... 3400 pounds
Empty weight (includes standard avionics) .... 2125 pounds
Useful load .... 1287 pounds

Stall speed (landing, full flaps) .... 59 MPH
Rate of climb at sea level .... 1167 feet per minute
Service ceiling .... 17,858 feet

Airspeed limits   Maneuvering .... 152 MPH
               Maximum structural cruising................ 190 MPH
               Never exceed............................ 225 MPH
               Flaps extended (normal) .... 140 MPH
               Landing gear extended (normal) .... 175 MPH
Fuel..................................... 100/130 octane minimum

The 1983 F33A Bonanza offered no change in exterior paint or the interior. Serial numbers began with CE-1014 and ended with CE-1023 . . . a total of 10 units, less than one airplane a month, the 1982 general aviation recession is now well on its way. Power Plant was again the Continental IO-520-BB rated at 285 H.P. The 1983 standard equipped price was $133,750.

THESE CHANGES OCCURRED DURING PRODUCTION:

- Improved static wick installation, CE-1026 and after,
- Standby generator disconnect, CE-1014 and after,
- Instrument panel laminate, woodgrain, CE-1012 and after.

F33A

BONANZA   **MODEL YEAR 1984**

Top speed at sea level . . . . 209 MPH
Maximum recommended cruise power . . . . 75% (214 HP)
Cruise speed at 75% power at 6000 feet (optimum altitude)
    full throttle, 2500 RPM . . . . 198 MPH
Standard fuel capacity . . . . 74 gallons
Maximum range (at 156 MPH at 10,000 feet)
    with standard tanks . . . . 894 miles
    (Range includes allowance for warm-up, taxi, takeoff, climb,
        and a 45-minute reserve at 45% power.)
Gross weight . . . . 3400 pounds
Empty weight (includes standard avionics) . . . . 2125 pounds
Useful load . . . . 1287 pounds

Stall speed (landing, full flaps) . . . . 59 MPH
Rate of climb at sea level . . . . 1167 feet per minute
Service ceiling . . . . 17,858 feet

Airspeed limits Maneuvering . . . . 152 MPH
                  Maximum structural cruising . . . . 190 MPH
                  Never exceed . . . . 225 MPH
                  Flaps extended (normal) . . . . 140 MPH
                  Landing gear extended (normal) . . . . 175 MPH
Fuel . . . . 100/130 octane minimum

1984 F33A Bonanza was the same as the 1983 F33A. Serial numbers were CE-1024, CE-1025, CE-1027 through CE-1032 . . . a total of only 8 units. The Power Plant was the Continental IO-520-BB rated at 285 H.P. The 1984 standard equipped price was $146,500.

THESE CHANGES OCCURRED DURING PRODUCTION:

- Optional approach plate holder, CE-1024 and after,
- Electro thermal propeller de-ice (Goodrich to McCauley) CE-1024 and after.

F33A

BONANZA   **MODEL YEAR 1985**

Top speed at sea level.................................. 209 MPH
Maximum recommended cruise power .... 75% (214 HP)
Cruise speed at 75% power at 6000 feet (optimum altitude)
    full throttle, 2500 RPM............................. 198 MPH
Standard fuel capacity..................................... 74 gallons
Maximum range (at 156 MPH at 10,000 feet)
    with standard tanks.................................. 894 miles
(Range includes allowance for warm-up, taxi, takeoff, climb,
    and a 45-minute reserve at 45% power.)
Gross weight .... 3400 pounds
Empty weight (includes standard avionics) .... 2125 pounds
Useful load .... 1287 pounds

Stall speed (landing, full flaps) ....59 MPH
Rate of climb at sea level .... 1167 feet per minute
Service ceiling .... 17,858 feet

Airspeed limits   Maneuvering .... 152 MPH
                Maximum structural cruising............... 190 MPH
                Never exceed........................... 225 MPH
                Flaps extended (normal) .... 140 MPH
                Landing gear extended (normal) .... 175 MPH
Fuel..................................... 100/130 octane minimum

Unchanged. The 1985 F33A Bonanza was the same as the four models preceding it. Serial numbers were CE-1026, CE-1033 through CE-1071 . . . a total of 40 units. The Power Plant was the Continental IO-520-BB rated at 285 H.P. The 1985 standard equipped price was $164,750.

THESE CHANGES OCCURRED DURING PRODUCTION:

- Improved engine manifold fuel drain, CE-1069 and after.

F33A
BONANZA

MODEL YEAR 1986

Top speed at sea level.................................... 209 MPH
Maximum recommended cruise power .... 75% (214 HP)
Cruise speed at 75% power at 6000 feet (optimum altitude)
    full throttle, 2500 RPM............................... 198 MPH
Standard fuel capacity..................................... 74 gallons
Maximum range (at 156 MPH at 10,000 feet)
    with standard tanks.................................. 894 miles
(Range includes allowance for warm-up, taxi, takeoff, climb,
     and a 45-minute reserve at 45% power.)
Gross weight .... 3400 pounds
Empty weight (includes standard avionics) .... 2113 pounds
Useful load .... 1299 pounds

Stall speed (landing, full flaps) .... 59 MPH
Rate of climb at sea level .... 1167 feet per minute
Service ceiling .... 17,858 feet

Airspeed limits Maneuvering .... 152 MPH
                Maximum structural cruising............... 190 MPH
                Never exceed........................... 225 MPH
                Flaps extended (normal) .... 140 MPH
                Landing gear extended (normal) .... 175 MPH
Fuel.................................... 100/130 octane minimum

Unchanged. The 1986 F33A Bonanza was essentially the same as the five models preceding it. Serial numbers began with CE-1072 and ended with CE-1101 . . . a total of 30 units. The Power Plant was the Continental IO-520-BB rated at 285 H.P. The 1986 standard equipped price was $164,750.

THESE CHANGES OCCURRED DURING PRODUCTION:

- Change to Slick magnetoes, CE-1076 and after,
- Flap and landing gear switch knob change, CE-1099.

F33A
BONANZA

MODEL YEAR 1987

Top speed at sea level . . . . 209 MPH
Maximum recommended cruise power . . . . 75% (214 HP)
Cruise speed at 75% power at 6000 feet (optimum altitude)
    full throttle, 2500 RPM . . . . 198 MPH
Standard fuel capacity . . . . 74 gallons
Maximum range (at 156 MPH at 10,000 feet)
    with standard tanks . . . . 894 miles
(Range includes allowance for warm-up, taxi, takeoff, climb,
      and a 45-minute reserve at 45% power.)
Gross weight . . . . 3400 pounds
Empty weight (includes standard avionics) . . . . 2227 pounds
Useful load . . . . 1185 pounds

Stall speed (landing, full flaps) . . . . 59 MPH
Rate of climb at sea level . . . . 1167 feet per minute
Service ceiling . . . . 17,858 feet

Airspeed limits Maneuvering . . . . 152 MPH
                 Maximum structural cruising . . . . 190 MPH
                 Never exceed . . . . 225 MPH
                 Flaps extended (normal) . . . . 140 MPH
                 Landing gear extended (normal) . . . . 175 MPH
Fuel . . . . 100/130 octane minimum

The big news about the 1987 F33A was that it was policy priced lower to attract more customers. The price dropped from $164,750 to $131,750, a decrease of $33,000. The policy worked . . . 105 units were sold. Serial numbers began with CE-1102 and ended with CE-1206. The Power Plant was the Continental IO-520-BB rated at 285 H.P. The interior and exterior remained unchanged from 1986.

THESE CHANGES OCCURRED DURING PRODUCTION:

- Instrument panel styling change, CE-1102 and after,
- Voltage regulator change, CE-1142 and after,
- Improved window seal, CE-1126 and after.

F33A

BONANZA

MODEL YEAR 1988

Top speed at sea level.................................... 209 MPH
Maximum recommended cruise power .... 75% (214 HP)
Cruise speed at 75% power at 6000 feet (optimum altitude)
    full throttle, 2500 RPM............................... 198 MPH
Standard fuel capacity.................................... 74 gallons
Maximum range (at 156 MPH at 10,000 feet)
    with standard tanks.................................. 894 miles
(Range includes allowance for warm-up, taxi, takeoff, climb,
    and a 45-minute reserve at 45% power.)
Gross weight .... 3400 pounds
Empty weight (includes standard avionics) .... 2237 pounds
Useful load .... 1175 pounds

Stall speed (landing, full flaps) .... 59 MPH
Rate of climb at sea level .... 1157 feet per minute
Service ceiling .... 17,858 feet

Airspeed limits   Maneuvering .... 152 MPH
                 Maximum structural cruising............... 190 MPH
                 Never exceed........................... 225 MPH
                 Flaps extended (normal) .... 140 MPH
                 Landing gear extended (normal) .... 175 MPH
Fuel.................................... 100/130 octane minimum

The 1988 F33A Bonanza was also policy priced at $135,750. The exterior and interior remained unchanged. Serial numbers began with CE-1207 and ended with CE-1306. The Power Plant was the Continental IO-520-BB rated at 285 H.P. 100 units were sold.

THESE CHANGES OCCURRED DURING PRODUCTION:

- Fuel boost pump vane improvement, CE-1238 and after,
- Change to Narco ELT, CE-1241 and after,
- Removal of sound deadener from firewall and adjacent skins, CE-1224 and after.

F33A
BONANZA

Top speed at sea level . . . . 209 MPH
Maximum recommended cruise power . . . . 75% (214 HP)
Cruise speed at 75% power at 6000 feet (optimum altitude)
    full throttle, 2500 RPM . . . . 198 MPH
Standard fuel capacity . . . . 74 gallons
Maximum range (at 156 MPH at 10,000 feet)
    with standard tanks . . . . 894 miles
(Range includes allowance for warm-up, taxi, takeoff, climb,
      and a 45-minute reserve at 45% power.)
Gross weight . . . . 3400 pounds
Empty weight (includes standard avionics) . . . . 2237 pounds
Useful load . . . . 59 pounds

Stall speed (landing, full flaps) . . . . 1175 MPH
Rate of climb at sea level . . . . 1157 feet per minute
Service ceiling . . . . 17,858 feet

Airspeed limits   Maneuvering . . . . 152 MPH
                  Maximum structural cruising . . . . 190 MPH
                  Never exceed . . . . 225 MPH
                  Flaps extended (normal) . . . . 140 MPH
                  Landing gear extended (normal) . . . . 175 MPH
Fuel . . . . 100/130 octane minimum

The 1989 F33A Bonanza was policy priced at $139,850. The exterior and interior remained unchanged. Serial numbers began with CE-1307 and ended with CE-1425 . . . 119 units. The Power Plant was the Continental IO-520-BB rated at 285 H.P.

THESE CHANGES OCCURRED DURING PRODUCTION:

- Exhaust air duct material change, CE-1422 and after,
- New fire extinguisher, CE-1387 and after,
- New cabin door latch placard, CE-1408 and after.

F33A

BONANZA

Top speed at sea level.................................... 209 MPH
Maximum recommended cruise power.................. 75% (214 HP)
Cruise speed at 75% power at 6000 feet (optimum altitude)
    full throttle, 2500 RPM............................... 198 MPH
Standard fuel capacity..................................... 74 gallons
Maximum range (at 156 MPH at 10,000 feet)
    with standard tanks.................................. 894 miles
(Range includes allowance for warm-up, taxi, takeoff, climb,
      and a 45-minute reserve at 45% power.)
Gross weight .... 3400 pounds
Empty weight (includes standard avionics) .... 2237 pounds
Useful load .... 1175 pounds

Stall speed (landing, full flaps) .... 59 MPH
Rate of climb at sea level .... 1157 feet per minute
Service ceiling .... 17,858 feet

Airspeed limits Maneuvering .... 152 MPH
               Maximum structural cruising............... 190 MPH
               Never exceed........................... 225 MPH
               Flaps extended (normal) .... 140 MPH
               Landing gear extended (normal) .... 175 MPH
Fuel .... 100/130 octane minimum

The 1990 F33A was policy priced at $154,650. The price increased to $156,000 at serial number CE-1456. The exterior and interior remained unchanged. Serial numbers began with CE-1426 and ended with CE-1549 . . . a total of 124 units. The Power Plant is the Continental IO-520-BB rated at 285 H.P.

THIS CHANGE IS OCCURRING DURING PRODUCTION:

- Change in instrument air regulator, CE-1440, CE-1457 and after.

F33C

BONANZA

MODEL YEAR 1973

At Utility Category Gross Weight

Top speed at sea level.................................... 208 MPH
Maximum recommended cruise power .... 75% (214 HP)
Cruise speed at 75% power at 6500 feet (optimum altitude)
    full throttle, 2500 RPM............................... 200 MPH
Standard fuel capacity..................................... 50 gallons
Maximum range (at 156 MPH at 10,000 feet)
    with standard tanks.................................... 595 miles
    with extended range tanks (80 gallons total) .... 1080 miles
(Ranges include an allowance for warm-up, taxi, takeoff, climb,
    and a 45-minute reserve at 45% power.)

	Utility Category	Acrobatic Category
Gross weight	3400 pounds	2800 pounds
Empty weight (includes standard avionics)	2000 pounds	1936 pounds
Useful load	1400 pounds	864 pounds

At Utility Category Gross Weight

Stall speed (landing, full flaps) ....63 MPH
Rate of climb at sea level .... 1136 feet per minute
Service ceiling ....17,500 feet

		Utility Category	Acrobatic Category
Airspeed limits	Maneuvering	152 MPH	165 MPH
	Maximum structural cruising	190 MPH	190 MPH
	Never exceed	225 MPH	234 MPH
	Flaps extended (normal)	140 MPH	140 MPH
	Landing gear extended (normal)	175 MPH	175 MPH

Fuel .... 100/130 octane minimum

The 1973 F33C Aerobatic Bonanza had two customers. The Iranian Air Force took eight airplanes, CJ-31 through CJ-38. Cutter Aviation, Phoenix, Arizona, took CJ-39. Power Plant was the Continental IO-520-BA rated at 285 H.P. The standard equipped price to the Iranians was $44,100. Cutter Aviation paid $48,000. A total of nine units.

THESE CHANGES OCCURRED DURING PRODUCTION:

- Standardization of landing gears, CJ-31 and after,
- Improved glareshield attachment, CJ-31 and after,
- Storm window seal improvement CJ-31 and after,
- New propeller governor CJ-31 and after,
- Improved Hartwell cowl latch handle, CJ-31 and after,
- Improved exhaust pipe support shock mounts, CJ-31 and after,
- Start relay circuit breaker, CJ-31 and after,
- Removal of mechanical nose gear position indicator, CJ-31 and after,
- Removal of nose gear guard assembly (wheel scraper), CJ-31 and after,
- Parking brake cable rerouting CJ-31 and after,
- Uplock roller grease bolt, main landing gear, CJ-31 and after,
- Engine damper pin change, CJ-31 and after,

- Standby generator, CJ-31 and after,
- Emergency locator transmitter, CJ-31 and after,
- New fuel quantity sensor, CJ-31 and after,
- One piece nose bug, CJ-31 and after,
- Elevator horn change, CJ-31 and after,
- Increase in unusable fuel, CJ-31 and after,
- Change to Bendix Model S6RN-1225 magnetos, CJ-31 and after,
- Control column drive change. CJ-31 and after,
- ELT bracket change, CJ-31 and after,
- New ELT antenna doubler, CJ-31 and after,
- Landing gear safety system pressure switch, CJ-31 and after,
- Aerobatic standard fuel system, CJ-31 and after,
- Additional seat track stops, CJ-31 and after.

F33C

BONANZA

At Utility Category Gross Weight

Top speed at sea level	208 MPH
Maximum recommended cruise power	75% (214 HP)
Cruise speed at 75% power at 6500 feet (optimum altitude) full throttle, 2500 RPM	200 MPH
Standard fuel capacity	44 gallons
Maximum range (at 156 MPH at 10,000 feet)	
with standard tanks	585 miles
with extended range tanks (74 gallons total)	895 miles

(Ranges include an allowance for warm-up, taxi, takeoff, climb, and a 45-minute reserve at 45% power.)

	Utility Category	Acrobatic Category
Gross weight	3400 pounds	2800 pounds
Empty weight (includes standard avionics)	2000 pounds	1936 pounds
Useful load	1400 pounds	864 pounds

At Utility Category Gross Weight

Stall speed (landing, full flaps)	63 MPH
Rate of climb at sea level	1136 feet per minute
Service ceiling	17,500 feet

		Utility Category	Acrobatic Category
Airspeed limits	Maneuvering	152 MPH	165 MPH
	Maximum structural cruising	190 MPH	190 MPH
	Never exceed	225 MPH	234 MPH
	Flaps extended (normal)	140 MPH	140 MPH
	Landing gear extended (normal)	175 MPH	175 MPH

Fuel . . . . 100/130 octane minimum

The 1974 F33C Aerobatic Bonanza had three customers. The Iranian Air Force took eleven airplanes, CJ-40 through CJ-51. The standard equipped price was $51,260. Spain took CJ-52, CJ-54, CJ-55, CJ-57 through CJ-61. The standard equipped price was $47,350. Cutter Aviation took CJ-53. The price was $55,270. The government of Mexico took CJ-62 and CJ-63. Their price was $47,350. The Power Plant was the Continental IO-520-BB rated at 285 H.P.

THESE CHANGES OCCURRED DURING PRODUCTION:

- Change to light twin engine floating panel attach brackets, CJ-40 and after,
- Openable window latching system improvement, CJ-40 and after,
- Chemical film treatment, exterior skins, CJ-40 and after,
- Improved sight gage installation, CJ-40 and after,
- Relocation of main landing gear torque knee lubricator, CJ-40 and after,
- Openable cabin window seal improvement, CJ-40 and after,
- Gust lock improvement, CJ-52 and after,
- Change to Hanlon-Wilson 701-20 muffler and a 701-21 heater muffler, CJ-52 and after,
- Change to 40 gallon fuel cell with bladder reservoir, CJ-40 and after,
- Aft cowl door handle, CJ-52 and after,
- Engine cowling reinforcement, CJ-44 and after,
- Heat and vent air flow improvement, CJ-52 and after,
- Rudder and aileron control cable interconnect clearance improvement, CJ-60 and after,
- Dual landing gear safety switch installation, CJ-62, CJ-63.

F33C
BONANZA

At Utility Category Gross Weight

Top speed at sea level	208 MPH
Maximum recommended cruise power	75% (214 HP)
Cruise speed at 75% power at 6500 feet (optimum altitude) full throttle, 2500 RPM	200 MPH
Standard fuel capacity	44 gallons
Maximum range (at 156 MPH at 10,000 feet)	
with standard tanks	585 miles
with extended range tanks (74 gallons total)	895 miles

(Ranges include an allowance for warm-up, taxi, takeoff, climb, and a 45-minute reserve at 45% power.)

	Utility Category	Acrobatic Category
Gross weight	3400 pounds	2800 pounds
Empty weight (includes standard avionics)	2076 pounds	1936 pounds
Useful load	1336 pounds	864 pounds

At Utility Category Gross Weight

Stall speed (landing, full flaps)	63 MPH
Rate of climb at sea level	1136 feet per minute
Service ceiling	17,500 feet

		Utility Category	Acrobatic Category
Airspeed limits	Maneuvering	152 MPH	165 MPH
	Maximum structural cruising	190 MPH	190 MPH
	Never exceed	225 MPH	234 MPH
	Flaps extended (normal)	140 MPH	140 MPH
	Landing gear extended (normal)	175 MPH	175 MPH

Fuel .... 100/130 octane minimum

The 1975 F33C Aerobatic Bonanza had seven customers. The Government of Mexico took CJ-64 through CJ-66, three units at a standard equipped price of $47,350; CJ-67 and CJ-68 went to the Spanish Air Ministry. The price was $47,350. CJ-69 through CJ-74 were again taken by the Government of Mexico at the same price of $47,350. The Spanish Air Ministry took CJ-75 and CJ-76. The price was again $47,350. The Government of Mexico jumped in again and took CJ-77 through CJ-85. The price was $47,350. The Iranian Air Force came back for CJ-86, the price was $57,250. Guatemala took CJ-87 at a price of $57,900. The Government of Haiti took CJ-88 for $58,175. C.Itoh and Company of Japan, picked up CJ-89 for $58,125. The Iranian Air Force came back and took delivery of CJ-90 through CJ-102, at a price of $52,029. Total deliveries for 1975 . . . 39 units. The Power Plant was the Continental IO-520-BA, rated at 285 H.P.

THESE CHANGES OCCURRED DURING PRODUCTION:

- Dual landing gear safety switch installation, CJ-64 through CJ-66, CJ-69 through CJ-74, CJ-77 and after,
- Rudder and aileron control cable interconnect clearance improvement, CJ-60 and after,
- Gust lock redesign, CJ-86 and after,
- Static wick material change, CJ-88 and after,
- Provisions for air conditioning installation, CJ-86 and after.

F33C

BONANZA   **MODEL YEAR 1976**

At Utility Category Gross Weight

Top speed at sea level.................................... 208 MPH
Maximum recommended cruise power ....75% (214 HP)
Cruise speed at 75% power at 6500 feet (optimum altitude)
    full throttle, 2500 RPM.............................. 200 MPH
Standard fuel capacity....................................44 gallons
Maximum range (at 156 MPH at 10,000 feet)
    with standard tanks.................................. 585 miles
    with extended range tanks (74 gallons total) .... 895 miles
(Ranges include an allowance for warm-up, taxi, takeoff, climb,
    and a 45-minute reserve at 45% power.)

	Utility Category	Acrobatic Category
Gross weight	3400 pounds	2800 pounds
Empty weight (includes standard avionics)	2076 pounds	1936 pounds
Useful load	1336 pounds	864 pounds

At Utility Category Gross Weight

Stall speed (landing, full flaps) ....63 MPH
Rate of climb at sea level .... 1136 feet per minute
Service ceiling ....17,500 feet

156

		Utility Category	Acrobatic Category
Airspeed limits	Maneuvering	152 MPH	165 MPH
	Maximum structural cruising	190 MPH	190 MPH
	Never exceed	225 MPH	234 MPH
	Flaps extended (normal)	130 MPH	130 MPH
	Landing gear extended (normal)	175 MPH	175 MPH

Fuel . . . . 100/130 octane minimum

The 1976 F33C Aerobatic Bonanzas had three customers. The Iranian Air Force took CJ-103 and CJ-104, at a price of $67,550. Aeromex Mexico, S.A. accepted delivery of CJ-105 through CJ-110 at a price of $67,550. Tecnavia Iberica, S.A. bought CJ-111 through CJ-128 for $69,163. A grand total of 26 units. All were powered by the Continental IO-520-BA, rated at 285 H.P.

THESE CHANGES OCCURRED DURING PRODUCTION:

- One piece frame cabin door quick release, CJ-111 and after.

F33C

BONANZA

MODEL YEAR 1977

At Utility Category Gross Weight

Top speed at sea level.................................... 209 MPH
Maximum recommended cruise power .... 75% (214 HP)
Cruise speed at 75% power at 6000 feet (optimum altitude)
    full throttle, 2500 RPM............................... 198 MPH
Standard fuel capacity..................................... 44 gallons
Maximum range (at 156 MPH at 10,000 feet)
    with standard tanks................................... 585 miles
    with extended range tanks (74 gallons total) .... 894 miles
(Ranges include an allowance for warm-up, taxi, takeoff, climb,
    and a 45-minute reserve at 45% power.)

	Utility Category	Acrobatic Category
Gross weight	3400 pounds	2800 pounds
Empty weight (includes standard avionics)	2112 pounds	1936 pounds
Useful load	1300 pounds	864 pounds

At Utility Category Gross Weight

Stall speed (landing, full flaps) .... 59 MPH
Rate of climb at sea level .... 1167 feet per minute
Service ceiling .... 17,858 feet

		Utility Category	Acrobatic Category
Airspeed limits	Maneuvering	152 MPH	165 MPH
	Maximum structural cruising	190 MPH	190 MPH
	Never exceed	225 MPH	234 MPH
	Flaps extended (normal)	140 MPH	140 MPH
	Landing gear extended (normal)	175 MPH	175 MPH

Fuel . . . . 100/130 octane minimum

The 1977 F33C Aerobatic Bonanza was a lonely critter. Only one was built for C. Itoh and Company, Japan. CJ-129 sold for $70,400. It was powered by the Continental IO-520-BA rated at 285 H.P.

THESE CHANGES OCCURRED DURING PRODUCTION:

- Improved pilot and copilot seat frame, CJ-129 and after,
- Oxygen mask containers, CJ-129 and after,
- Airspeed indicator change, knots on the outside, CJ-129 and after,
- Dual brake plumbing routing change, CJ-129 and after,
- Quartz digital chronometer, CJ-129 and after,
- Standby generator functional test, CJ-129 and after,
- Pilot and passenger shoulder restraints, CJ-129 and after.

F33C

BONANZA

At Utility Category Gross Weight

Top speed at sea level	209 MPH
Maximum recommended cruise power	75% (214 HP)

Cruise speed at 75% power at 6000 feet (optimum altitude)

full throttle, 2500 RPM	198 MPH
Standard fuel capacity	44 gallons

Maximum range (at 156 MPH at 10,000 feet)

with standard tanks	585 miles
with extended range tanks (74 gallons total)	894 miles

(Ranges include an allowance for warm-up, taxi, takeoff, climb, and a 45-minute reserve at 45% power.)

	Utility Category	Acrobatic Category
Gross weight	3400 pounds	2800 pounds
Empty weight (includes standard avionics)	2107 pounds	1936 pounds
Useful load	1305 pounds	864 pounds

At Utility Category Gross Weight

Stall speed (landing, full flaps)	59 MPH
Rate of climb at sea level	1167 feet per minute
Service ceiling	17,858 feet

		Utility Category	Acrobatic Category
Airspeed limits	Maneuvering	152 MPH	165 MPH
	Maximum structural cruising	190 MPH	190 MPH
	Never exceed	225 MPH	234 MPH
	Flaps extended (normal)	140 MPH	140 MPH
	Landing gear extended (normal)	175 MPH	175 MPH
Fuel		100/130 octane minimum	

The 1978 F33C Aerobatic Bonanza had five customers. CJ-130 through CJ-141 were delivered to The Netherlands Flying Service at $70,400 each. CJ-142 was bought by Ohio Aviation, Dayton, Ohio for $76,500. CJ-143 was purchased by Houston Beechcraft, Houston, Texas, for $76,500. CJ-144 went to Experimental Engineering and was later flown with winglets. They didn't work. CJ-145 through CJ-148 were bought by The Netherlands Flying School for $76,525 each. A total of 19 units. All were powered by the Continental IO-520-BA Rated at 285 H.P.

THESE CHANGES OCCURRED DURING PRODUCTION:

- New seal for openable windows, CJ-141 and after,
- Corrosion preventative treatment, CJ-130 and after,
- Shuttle valve change — dual brakes, CJ-139 and after.

161

F33C

BONANZA

MODEL YEAR 1979

At Utility Category Gross Weight

Top speed at sea level . . . . 209 MPH
Maximum recommended cruise power . . . . 75% (214 HP)
Cruise speed at 75% power at 6000 feet (optimum altitude)
    full throttle, 2500 RPM . . . . 198 MPH
Standard fuel capacity . . . . 44 gallons
Maximum range (at 156 MPH at 10,000 feet)
    with standard tanks . . . . 585 miles
    with extended range tanks (74 gallons total) . . . . 894 miles
(Ranges include an allowance for warm-up, taxi, takeoff, climb,
    and a 45-minute reserve at 45% power.)

	Utility Category	Acrobatic Category
Gross weight	3400 pounds	2800 pounds
Empty weight (includes standard avionics)	2113 pounds	1936 pounds
Useful load	1299 pounds	864 pounds

At Utility Category Gross Weight

Stall speed (landing, full flaps) . . . . 59 MPH
Rate of climb at sea level . . . . 1167 feet per minute
Service ceiling . . . . 17,858 feet

		Utility Category	Acrobatic Category
Airspeed limits	Maneuvering	152 MPH	165 MPH
	Maximum structural cruising	190 MPH	190 MPH
	Never exceed	225 MPH	234 MPH
	Flaps extended (normal)	140 MPH	140 MPH
	Landing gear extended (normal)	175 MPH	175 MPH
Fuel .... 100/130 octane minimum			

The 1979 F33C Aerobatic Bonanza had two customers. CJ-149 went to The Netherlands Flying Service. The price was $85,162. CJ-150 through CJ-155 were bought by Transair France at a price of $88,000. A total of seven units. All were powered by the Continental IO-520-BB rated at 285 H.P.

THESE CHANGES OCCURRED DURING PRODUCTION:

- Pilot and copilot shoulder restraints, CJ-149 and after,
- Tail nav/strobe light change, CJ-150 and after,
- Torque adjusting sunvisor, CJ-149 and after,
- 28-volt propeller de-ice, CJ-151 and after,
- Approach flap position on flap switch CJ-150 and after,
- Shuttle valve change, dual brake system, CJ-149 and after,
- TCM 100 AMP alternator, CJ-150 and after,
- Series plumbing for dual brakes, CJ-150 and after,
- Floating panel bonding strap, CJ-150 and after,
- Improved openable window sealing, CJ-149 and after,
- Liquid crystal digital clock, CJ-150 and after.

F33C
BONANZA

MODEL YEAR 1986

At Utility Category Gross Weight

Top speed at sea level.................................... 209 MPH
Maximum recommended cruise power .... 75% (214 HP)
Cruise speed at 75% power at 6000 feet (optimum altitude)
    full throttle, 2500 RPM............................... 198 MPH
Standard fuel capacity..................................... 74 gallons
Maximum range (at 156 MPH at 10,000 feet)
    with standard tanks.................................. 894 miles
(Range includes an allowance for warm-up, taxi, takeoff, climb,
    and a 45-minute reserve at 45% power.)

	Utility Category	Acrobatic Category
Gross weight	3400 pounds	2800 pounds
Empty weight (includes standard avionics)	2113 pounds	1936 pounds
Useful load	1299 pounds	864 pounds

At Utility Category Gross Weight

Stall speed (landing, full flaps) .... 59 MPH
Rate of climb at sea level .... 1167 feet per minute
Service ceiling .... 17,858 feet

		Utility Category	Acrobatic Category
Airspeed limits	Maneuvering	152 MPH	165 MPH
	Maximum structural cruising	190 MPH	190 MPH
	Never exceed	225 MPH	234 MPH
	Flaps extended (normal)	140 MPH	140 MPH
	Landing gear extended (normal)	175 MPH	175 MPH

Fuel .... 100/130 octane minimum

The 1986 F33C Aerobatic Bonanza had three customers. CJ-156 through CJ-176 went to the National Ministry of Defense of Mexico. The price was $175,600. Maine Beechcraft took CJ-172 at a price of $175,600. CJ-178 went to Beechcraft East, Farmingdale, New York, for a standard list price of $175,600. A total of 23 units. All were powered by the Continental IO-520-BB rated at 285 H.P.

Beginning with CJ-156, all Aerobatic Bonanzas received vortex generators on each wing leading edge to hasten spin recovery. The earlier Aerobatic Bonanzas received the same generators by way of a factory retrofit kit. In addition to hastening spin recovery, the vortex generators produced a very gentle stall break. The vortex generators were also used on the 1984 A36 and B36 TC and succeeding models.

THESE CHANGES OCCURRED DURING PRODUCTION:

- Duct installation, cabin air exhaust drain, CJ-156 and after,
- Improved dynamic brake relay, CJ-156 and after,
- New voltage regulator, CJ-156 and after,
- Reduced aileron freeplay, CJ-156 and after,
- Airspeed indicator with approach flap white triangle, CJ-156 and after,
- 60 AMP Teledyne Crittenden alternator, CJ-156 and after,
- External power relay control, CJ-156 and after,
- 1980 noise level reduction, CJ-156 and after,
- 80 gallon fuel system as standard equipment, CJ-156 and after,
- Temperature improved liquid crystal digital clock, CJ-156 and after,
- Longer control column assembly, CJ-156 and after,
- Turn coordinator with power warning indicator, CJ-156 and after,
- Collins power converter, CJ-156 and after,
- Openable window latch improvement, CJ-156 and after,

- Narco ELT installation, CJ-156 and after,
- Aersonic fuel flow system, CJ-156 and after,
- New engine winter baffles, CJ-156 and after,
- New static wick installation, CJ-156 and after,
- Improved openable window latch mechanism, CJ-156 and after,
- Standard aircraft corrosion proofing, CJ-156 and after,
- Propeller de-ice installation, CJ-156 and after,
- Improved static wick installation CJ-156 and after,
- Standby generator disconnect, CJ-156 and after,
- Improved engine manifold fuel drain, CJ-156 and after,
- Improved fuel reservoir assembly, CJ-156 and after,
- Optional fresh air blower installation, CJ-156 and after,
- Improved alternator voltage regulator, CJ-156 and after,
- Change to Slick mangetoes, CJ-156 and after.

F33C

BONANZA   **MODEL YEAR 1987**

At Utility Category Gross Weight

Top speed at sea level..................................... 209 MPH
Maximum recommended cruise power.................. 75% (214 HP)
Cruise speed at 75% power at 6000 feet (optimum altitude)
    full throttle, 2500 RPM............................... 198 MPH
Standard fuel capacity..................................... 74 gallons
Maximum range (at 156 MPH at 10,000 feet)
    with standard tanks.................................. 894 miles
(Range includes an allowance for warm-up, taxi, takeoff, climb,
    and a 45-minute reserve at 45% power.)

	Utility Category	Acrobatic Category
Gross weight	3400 pounds	2800 pounds
Empty weight (includes standard avionics)	2113 pounds	1936 pounds
Useful load	1299 pounds	864 pounds

At Utility Category Gross Weight

Stall speed (landing, full flaps) .... 59 MPH
Rate of climb at sea level .... 1167 feet per minute
Service ceiling .... 17,858 feet

		Utility Category	Acrobatic Category
Airspeed limits	Maneuvering	152 MPH	165 MPH
	Maximum structural cruising	190 MPH	190 MPH
	Never exceed	225 MPH	234 MPH
	Flaps extended (normal)	140 MPH	140 MPH
	Landing gear extended (normal)	175 MPH	175 MPH

Fuel . . . . 100/130 octane minimum

The 1987 F33C Aerobatic Bonanza was another lonely critter. Only one was built. It went to Stevens Aviation, Greer, South Carolina. CJ-179 had a standard equipped price of $184,500. It was powered by the Continental IO-520-BB rated at 285 H.P.

THIS WAS THE ONLY CHANGE THAT OCCURRED ON THIS ONE UNIT:

- Improved window seal, CJ-179.

G33

BONANZA

Top speed at sea level.................................... 204 MPH
Maximum recommended cruise power .... 75% (195 HP)
Cruise speed at 75% power at 7000 feet (optimum altitude)
    full throttle, 2450 RPM............................... 193 MPH
Standard fuel capacity..................................... 50 gallons
Maximum range (at 156 MPH at 10,000 feet)
    with standard tanks................................. 680 miles
    with extended range tanks (80 gallons total) .... 1243 miles
(Ranges include an allowance for warm-up, taxi, takeoff, climb,
    and a 45-minute reserve at 45% power.)
Gross weight .... 3300 pounds
Empty weight.. 1935 pounds
Useful load .... 1365 pounds

Stall speed (landing, full flaps) .... 57 MPH
Rate of climb at sea level .... 1060 feet per minute
Service ceiling .... 16,600 feet

Airspeed limits   Maneuvering .... 152 MPH
               Maximum structural cruising............... 190 MPH
               Never exceed.......................... 225 MPH
               Flaps extended (normal) .... 140 MPH
               Landing gear extended (normal) .... 175 MPH
Fuel.................................... 100/130 octane minimum

The 1972 G33 was introduced to the Bonanza line to fill the market gap vacated by the F33 during 1970. Biggest single change is additional power. The G33 uses the Continental IO-470-N which develops 260 horsepower maximum continuous at 2625 RPM. This engine was last used on the 1963 P35 Bonanza. Its installation in the G33 differs in this respect, however, it's canted in the same way as the IO-520-B used in the other Bonanzas — two degrees down and two and one-half degrees to the right — less rudder power is required during takeoff and climb out, and there is improvement in longitudinal stability. Another difference is that a 60 amp alternator is used, rather than a 50 amp generator.

The first G33 is CD-1255 which was manufactured in 1971 as the production prototype. This unit has a 1971 interior. All other G33s have the interior improvements common to the rest of the 1972 Bonanza line, more headroom, restyling of interior, chairs, instrument panel, and an improved overhead fresh air system.

The gross weight is 250 pounds higher than the F33 and all other performance is increased.

CD-1256 is the first 1972 G33. CD-1299 was the last. The price was $41,450. Total number produced . . . 45 units.

THESE CHANGES OCCURRED DURING PRODUCTION:

- Standardization with other Bonanzas by using the same wheels and tires, CD-1272 and after,
- Replace Goodyear wheels and brakes with Cleveland wheels and brakes, CD-1299 and after,
- Improved exhaust pipe support shock mounts, CD-1299 and after,
- Parking brake control cable routing change, CD-1274 and after,
- Zerk fitting placed in uplock roller grease bolt on main landing gear, CD-1257 and after,

- Optional standby generator, CD-1290 and after,
- Robin Tech engine mounts replaced by Lord engine mounts for smoother operation, CD-1255 and after,
- Emergency locator transmitter, CD-1255 and after,
- Baffled fuel cells, CD-1274 and after,
- Improved fuel quantity sensors, CD-1265 and after,
- One piece nose bug for better cowling fit, CD-1297 and after,
- Hartzell two blade propeller, CD-1284,
- Increased unusable fuel by six gallons, CD-1277 and after,
- Bendix Model 1225 magnetos replaced Slick magnetos, CD-1293 and after,
- New E.L.T. doubler to reduce vibration, CD-1296 and after.

G33

BONANZA

MODEL YEAR 1973

Top speed at sea level	204 MPH
Maximum recommended cruise power	75% (195 HP)
Cruise speed at 75% power at 7000 feet (optimum altitude) full throttle, 2450 RPM	193 MPH
Standard fuel capacity	50 gallons
Maximum range (at 156 MPH at 10,000 feet) with standard tanks	680 miles
with extended range tanks (80 gallons total)	1243 miles

(Ranges include an allowance for warm-up, taxi, takeoff, climb, and a 45-minute reserve at 45% power.)

Gross weight	3300 pounds
Empty weight (includes standard avionics)	1935 pounds
Useful load	1365 pounds
Stall speed (landing, full flaps)	57 MPH
Rate of climb at sea level	1060 feet per minute
Service ceiling	16,600 feet

Airspeed limits		
	Maneuvering	152 MPH
	Maximum structural cruising	190 MPH
	Never exceed	225 MPH
	Flaps extended (normal)	140 MPH
	Landing gear extended (normal)	175 MPH
Fuel		100/130 octane minimum

Virtually the same airplane as the 1972 model. Only five units were produced, CD-1300 through CD-1304. The price remained at $41,450.

THESE CHANGES OCCURRED DURING PRODUCTION:

- Control column drive chain change from a "silent" chain to a "roller" chain, CD-1300 and after,
- Additional seat track stops, CD-1302 and after.

A36

BONANZA

MODEL YEAR 1972

Top speed at sea level . . . . 204 MPH
Maximum recommended cruise power . . . . 75% (214 HP)
Cruise speed at 75% power at 6500 feet (optimum altitude)
    full throttle, 2500 RPM . . . . 195 MPH
Standard fuel capacity . . . . 50 gallons
Maximum range (at 167 MPH at 10,000 feet)
    with standard tanks . . . . 530 miles
    with extended range tanks (80 gallons total) . . . . 980 miles
(Ranges include allowance for warm-up, taxi, takeoff, climb,
    and a 45-minute reserve at 45% power.)
Gross weight . . . . 3600 pounds
Empty weight (includes standard avionics) . . . . 2040 pounds
Useful load . . . . 1560 pounds

Stall speed (landing, full flaps) . . . . 64 MPH
Rate of climb at sea level . . . . 1015 feet per minute
Service ceiling . . . . 16,000 feet

Airspeed limits   Maneuvering . . . . 160 MPH
                 Maximum structural cruising . . . . 190 MPH
                 Never exceed . . . . 234 MPH
                 Flaps extended (normal) . . . . 140 MPH
                 Landing gear extended (normal) . . . . 175 MPH
Fuel . . . . 100/130 octane minimum

Here again no change in model designation, but the 1972 A36 received the same new interior treatment accorded the other 1972 Bonanzas. Cabin chairs and the instrument panel were restyled, and there is additional head room. The overhead ventilation system was also redesigned to bring in more fresh air and to bring it in quieter. Another significant development is the change to the all electric vertical readout engine instruments previously introduced on the 1971 V35B. The 1972 A36 has a new paint design to identify it from earlier models. Empty weight is up slightly over that of the 1971 A36, otherwise performance is unchanged. Power Plant was the Continental IO-520-BA rated at 285 H.P.

Serials of the 1972 A36 production start with E-283. The price was initially $45,550, but was later increased to $50,500. The last serial number is E-363, for a total of 81 units.

THESE CHANGES OCCURRED DURING PRODUCTION:

- Elevator horn change, E-362 and after,
- Flap shaft and landing gear retract rod clearance improvement, E-344 and after,
- Increase in unusable fuel, CE-311 and after,
- Bendix Model S6RN-1225 magnetos, E-287, E-347 and after,
- Control column drive change, E-363 and after,
- ELT bracket change, E-361 and after,
- New radio shelf assembly, E-335 and after,
- New ELT antenna doubler, E-351 and after,
- Edo-Aire Mitchell Century I flight control system, E-339 and after.

A36
BONANZA

Top speed at sea level................................... 204 MPH

Maximum recommended cruise power .... 75% (214 HP)

Cruise speed at 75% power at 6500 feet (optimum altitude)
    full throttle, 2500 RPM............................. 196 MPH

Standard fuel capacity..................................... 44 gallons

Maximum range (at 167 MPH at 10,000 feet)
    with standard tanks.................................. 530 miles
    with extended range tanks (74 gallons total) .... 863 miles
(Ranges include allowance for warm-up, taxi, takeoff, climb,
    and a 45-minute reserve at 45% power.)

Gross weight .... 3600 pounds

Empty weight (includes standard avionics) .... 2040 pounds

Useful load .... 1560 pounds

Stall speed (landing, full flaps) .... 63 MPH

Rate of climb at sea level .... 1015 feet per minute

Service ceiling .... 16,000 feet

Airspeed limits   Maneuvering .... 160 MPH
                 Maximum structural cruising............... 190 MPH
                 Never exceed.......................... 234 MPH
                 Flaps extended (normal) .... 140 MPH
                 Landing gear extended (normal) .... 175 MPH

Fuel.................................... 100/130 octane minimum

Unchanged. The 1973 A36 had the same interior and exterior paint design as the 1972 model. Serial numbers were E-364 through E-476 . . . a total of 81 units. The Power Plant was the Continental IO-520-BA rated at 285 H.P. The 1973 standard equipped price was $50,500.

THESE CHANGES OCCURRED DURING PRODUCTION:

- Discontinued vertical instruments, replaced by Edo-Aire wet line cluster, E-364 and after,
- New ELT antenna installation, E-377 and after,
- Openable window latching system improvement, E-390 and after,
- Additional seat track stops, E-372 through E-379,
- Chemical film treatment — exterior skins, E-450 and after,
- New marker beacon antenna for 1973, E-364 and after,
- Relocation of optional fifth ash tray, E-398 and after,
- Improved air pump filter, E-452 and after,
- Addition of fuel cell drain spacer, E-398 and after,
- Improved fuel sight gage installation, E-382 and after,
- Relocation of main landing gear torque knee lubrication, E-423 and after,
- Openable cabin window seal improvement, E-410 and after,
- Adjustable nose gear brace assembly, E-437 and after,
- Additional seat track stops, E-380 and after,
- Center foot change on pilot and copilot seats, E-421 and after,
- Landing gear retract rod end improvement, E-443 and after,
- Seat back support change (aft facing), E-435 and after,
- Improved gust lock, E-465 and after,
- Aft cowl door handle, E-475 and after.

A36

BONANZA   MODEL YEAR 1974

Top speed at sea level.................................... 204 MPH
Maximum recommended cruise power.................. 75% (214 HP)
Cruise speed at 75% power at 6500 feet (optimum altitude)
    full throttle, 2500 RPM............................... 196 MPH
Standard fuel capacity..................................... 44 gallons
Maximum range (at 167 MPH at 10,000 feet)
    with standard tanks.................................... 530 miles
    with extended range tanks (74 gallons total)............. 863 miles
(Ranges include allowance for warm-up, taxi, takeoff, climb,
    and a 45-minute reserve at 45% power.)
Gross weight .... 3600 pounds
Empty weight (includes standard avionics) .... 2096 pounds
Useful load .... 1516 pounds

Stall speed (landing, full flaps) .... 60 MPH
Rate of climb at sea level .... 1015 feet per minute
Service ceiling .... 16,000 feet

Airspeed limits   Maneuvering .... 160 MPH
                Maximum structural cruising............... 190 MPH
                Never exceed........................... 234 MPH
                Flaps extended (normal) .... 140 MPH
                Landing gear extended (normal) .... 175 MPH
Fuel.................................... 100/130 octane minimum

The 1974 A36 Bonanza had a new interior and exterior paint design. Serial numbers were E-477 through E-604 . . . a total of 128 units. The Power Plant was the Continental IO-520-BA rated at 285 H.P. The 1974 standard equipped price was $52,000.

THESE CHANGES OCCURRED DURING PRODUCTION:

- Hanlon-Wilson 701-20 muffler and 701-21 heater muffler, E-488 and after,
- Improved fuel quantity printed circuit breaker, E-505 and after,
- Engine cowling reinforcement, E-495 and after,
- ELT change (narrow band), E-485 and after,
- Altimeter out sensor shunt resistor, E-538 and after,
- Heat and vent airflow improvement, E-576 and after,
- Strobe light grounding improvement, E-582 and after,
- Rudder and aileron control cable interconnect clearance improvement, E-604 and after.

A36

BONANZA

Top speed at sea level. . . . . 204 MPH

Maximum recommended cruise power . . . . 75% (214 HP)

Cruise speed at 75% power at 6500 feet (optimum altitude)
     full throttle, 2500 RPM. . . . . 195 MPH

Standard fuel capacity. . . . . 44 gallons

Maximum range (at 167 MPH at 10,000 feet)
     with standard tanks. . . . . 530 miles
     with extended range tanks (74 gallons total) . . . . 863 miles

(Ranges include allowance for warm-up, taxi, takeoff, climb,
     and a 45-minute reserve at 45% power.)

Gross weight . . . . 3600 pounds

Empty weight (includes standard avionics) . . . . 2111 pounds

Useful load . . . . 1501 pounds

Stall speed (landing, full flaps) . . . . 60 MPH

Rate of climb at sea level . . . . 1015 feet per minute

Service ceiling . . . . 16,000 feet

Airspeed limits   Maneuvering . . . . 160 MPH
                   Maximum structural cruising. . . . . 190 MPH
                   Never exceed. . . . . 234 MPH
                   Flaps extended (normal) . . . . 140 MPH
                   Landing gear extended (normal) . . . . 175 MPH

Fuel. . . . . 100/130 octane minimum

The 1975 A36 Bonanza was unchanged from the 1974 model. Serial numbers were E-605 through E-765 . . . a total of 161 units. The Power Plant was the Continental IO-520-BA rated at 285 H.P. The 1975 standard equipped price was $59,000.

THESE CHANGES OCCURRED DURING PRODUCTION:

- Redesigned gust lock, E-619 and after,
- Dual landing gear safety switch installation, E-606 and after,
- Improved shoulder harness lap belt, E-605 and after,
- Improved overhead console radio speaker, E-617 and after,
- Material change in static wick discharge, E-674 and after,
- Hydraulic brake plumbing routing improvement, E-639 and after,
- Extended seat track travel, E-632 and after,
- Explosion containing strobe light, E-604, E-608 and after,
- Utility door stop assembly change, E-681 and after,
- Addition of nose side skin stiffeners, E-601 and after,
- Provisions for air conditioning installation, E-687 and after,
- Improved cabin door windlace, E-611 and after,
- Optional air conditioning available, E-732 and after,
- Landing gear activator worm shaft, bushing, and bearing change, E-701 and after,
- IO-520-BA spec 12 engine, E-686 and after,
- Elevator tab bracket change, E-650 and after,
- Forward utility door support bracket change, E-661 and after,
- Utility door and cabin door inside handle improvement, E-665 and after,
- Barry engine mounts, E-678, E-679, E-680 only,
- IO-520-BA spec 10 engine with Slick magnetos (662), E-651, E-665 only,
- Hat shelf installation, E-653 and after,
- Electro mech landing gear motor, E-748 and after,
- Elevator trim tab activator tube assembly change, E-739 and after.

MODEL YEAR 1976

Top speed at sea level.................................... 204 MPH
Maximum recommended cruise power .... 75% (214 HP)
Cruise speed at 75% power at 6500 feet (optimum altitude)
    full throttle, 2500 RPM............................... 196 MPH
Standard fuel capacity..................................... 44 gallons
Maximum range (at 167 MPH at 10,000 feet)
    with standard tanks................................... 530 miles
    with extended range tanks (74 gallons total) .... 863 miles
(Ranges include allowance for warm-up, taxi, takeoff, climb,
    and a 45-minute reserve at 45% power.)
Gross weight .... 3600 pounds
Empty weight (includes standard avionics) .... 2111 pounds
Useful load .... 1501 pounds

Stall speed (landing, full flaps) ....60 MPH
Rate of climb at sea level .... 1015 feet per minute
Service ceiling .... 16,000 feet

Airspeed limits   Maneuvering .... 160 MPH
                 Maximum structural cruising............... 190 MPH
                 Never exceed........................... 234 MPH
                 Flaps extended (normal) .... 140 MPH
                 Landing gear extended (normal) .... 175 MPH
Fuel.................................... 100/130 octane minimum

The 1976 A36 Bonanza had a new interior but the exterior paint design remained the same as the 1975 model. Serial numbers were E-766 through E-926 . . . 161 units. The Power Plant was the Continental IO-520-BA rated at 285 H.P. The 1976 standard equipped price was $65,950.

THESE CHANGES OCCURRED DURING PRODUCITON:

- Improved seat foot casting, E-892 and after,
- Bonded cowling doors, E-862 and E-941 only,
- Improved cabin reading lights, E-904 and after,
- Aft cabin door stop — forward utility door, E-911 and after,
- Pilot and copilot shoulder restraints, E-825 and after,
- One piece cabin door frame, E-831 and after.

A36

BONANZA

MODEL YEAR 1977

Top speed at sea level . . . . 206 MPH
Maximum recommended cruise power . . . . 75% (214 HP)
Cruise speed at 75% power at 6000 feet (optimum altitude)
    full throttle, 2500 RPM . . . . 193 MPH
Standard fuel capacity . . . . 44 gallons
Maximum range (at 167 MPH at 10,000 feet)
    with standard tanks . . . . 530 miles
    with extended range tanks (74 gallons total) . . . . 861 miles
(Ranges include allowance for warm-up, taxi, takeoff, climb,
      and a 45-minute reserve at 45% power.)
Gross weight . . . . 3600 pounds
Empty weight (includes standard avionics) . . . . 2157 pounds
Useful load . . . . 1455 pounds

Stall speed (landing, full flaps) . . . . 60 MPH
Rate of climb at sea level . . . . 1030 feet per minute
Service ceiling . . . . 16,600 feet

Airspeed limits   Maneuvering . . . . 160 MPH
                 Maximum structural cruising . . . . 190 MPH
                 Never exceed . . . . 234 MPH
                 Flaps extended (normal) . . . . 140 MPH
                 Landing gear extended (normal) . . . . 175 MPH
Fuel . . . . 100/130 octane minimum

The 1977 A36 Bonanza had a new exterior paint design. Serial numbers were E-927 through E-1151, except E-1111 . . . a total of 224 units. The Power Plant was the Continental IO-520-BA rated at 285 H.P. The 1977 standard equipped price was $70,550.

THESE CHANGES OCCURRED DURING PRODUCTION:

- Shoulder harness inertia reels, E-937 and after,
- Improved pilot and copilot seat frames, E-939 and after,
- Oxygen mask containers, E-927 and after,
- Fifth and sixth seat design improvement, E-939 and after,
- Airspeed indicator change — knots on the outside, E-927 and after,
- Inertia reel relocation, E-1048 and after,
- Baggage net improvement, E-927 and after,
- Improved air conditioning pressure relief valve, E-963 and after,
- Dual brake plumbing routing change, E-1031 and after,
- Air conditioning condenser fairing change, E-1151 and after,
- 24-volt electrical system, E-1111,
- Quartz digital chronometer, E-1059 and after,
- Corrosion preventative treatment of elevator control push rods, E-1134 and after,
- Standby generator functional test, E-1078 and after,
- Overhead fresh air valve assembly change, E-1091 and after,
- Brake plumbing change, E-1062 and after.

A36
BONANZA

Top speed at sea level.................................... 206 MPH
Maximum recommended cruise power.................. 75% (214 HP)
Cruise speed at 75% power at 6000 feet (optimum altitude)
    full throttle, 2500 RPM............................... 193 MPH
Standard fuel capacity..................................... 44 gallons
Maximum range (at 167 MPH at 10,000 feet)
    with standard tanks.................................... 530 miles
    with extended range tanks (74 gallons total)............. 861 miles
(Ranges include allowance for warm-up, taxi, takeoff, climb,
    and a 45-minute reserve at 45% power.)
Gross weight .... 3600 pounds
Empty weight (includes standard avionics) .... 2148 pounds
Useful load .... 1464 pounds

Stall speed (landing, full flaps) .... 60 MPH
Rate of climb at sea level .... 1030 feet per minute
Service ceiling .... 16,600 feet

Airspeed limits   Maneuvering .... 160 MPH
                  Maximum structural cruising............... 190 MPH
                  Never exceed............................ 234 MPH
                  Flaps extended (normal) .... 140 MPH
                  Landing gear extended (normal) .... 175 MPH
Fuel..................................... 100/130 octane minimum

The 1978 A36 Bonanza had a restyled interior but the same exterior paint design as the 1977 model. Serial numbers were E-1111, E-1152 through E-1370 . . . a total of 220 units. The Power Plant was the Continental IO-520-BA rated at 285 H.P. The 1978 standard equipped price was $77,550.

THESE CHANGES OCCURRED DURING PRODUCTION:

- Defroster duct redesign, E-1162 and after,
- Strobe wiring relocation, E-1230 and after,
- Trim tab actuator change, E-1152 and after,
- New improved seals for openable windows, E-1212 and after,
- Dual brakes shuttle valve change, E-1204 and after,
- Torque adjusting sunvisor, E-1344 and after,
- 28-volt propeller de-ice, E-1255, E-1288 and after,
- Oxygen bottle installation, E-1370 and after,
- Freon compressor change E-1231 and after.

A36
BONANZA

MODEL YEAR 1979

Top speed at sea level . . . . 206 MPH
Maximum recommended cruise power . . . . 75% (214 HP)
Cruise speed at 75% power at 6000 feet (optimum altitude)
    full throttle, 2500 RPM . . . . 193 MPH
Standard fuel capacity . . . . 44 gallons
Maximum range (at 167 MPH at 10,000 feet)
    with standard tanks . . . . 530 miles
    with extended range tanks (74 gallons total) . . . . 861 miles
(Ranges include allowance for warm-up, taxi, takeoff, climb,
    and a 45-minute reserve at 45% power.)
Gross weight . . . . 3600 pounds
Empty weight (includes standard avionics) . . . . 2161 pounds
Useful load . . . . 1451 pounds

Stall speed (landing, full flaps) . . . . 60 MPH
Rate of climb at sea level . . . . 1030 feet per minute
Service ceiling . . . . 16,600 feet

Airspeed limits   Maneuvering . . . . 160 MPH
                  Maximum structural cruising . . . . 190 MPH
                  Never exceed . . . . 234 MPH
                  Flaps extended (normal) . . . . 140 MPH
                  Landing gear extended (normal) . . . . 175 MPH
Fuel . . . . 100/130 octane minimum

The 1979 A36 Bonanza had a restyled interior but the same exterior paint design as the 1978 model. Serial numbers were E-1371 through E-1593 . . . 223 units. The Power Plant was the Continental IO-520-BB rated at 285 H.P. The 1979 standard equipped price was $88,000.

THESE CHANGES OCCURRED DURING PRODUCTION:

- Approach flap position on flap switch, E-1371 and after,
- Standby generator — 28 volts, E-1424 and after,
- Emergency exit placard improvement, E-1371 and after,
- Aileron control rod assembly bearing improvement, E-1408 through E-1411 only,
- TCM 100 AMP alternator made available, E-1519 and after,
- Landing gear limit switch adjustment, E-1439 and after,
- Series plumbing for dual brakes, E-1432 and after,
- Engine venturi intake valves, E-1422, E-1450, E-1457, E-1460, E-1461, E-1464, E-1465, E-1466, E-1471, E-1473 through E-1503, E-1505, E-1514, E-1515, E-1517 and after,
- Floating panel bonding strap, E-1502 and after,
- Improved openable window seals, E-1455 and after,
- Radar antenna installation, E-1534, E-1537 and after,
- Lower rotating beacon connector addition, E-1552 and after,
- Openable window latch improvement, E-1422, E-1551, E-1569, E-1581, E-1594 and after.

A36
BONANZA

MODEL YEAR 1980

Top speed at sea level . . . . 206 MPH
Maximum recommended cruise power . . . . 75% (214 HP)
Cruise speed at 75% power at 6000 feet (optimum altitude)
     full throttle, 2500 RPM . . . . 193 MPH
Standard fuel capacity . . . . 74 gallons
Maximum range (at 167 MPH at 10,000 feet)
     with standard tanks . . . . 861 miles
(Range includes allowance for warm-up, taxi, takeoff, climb,
     and a 45-minute reserve at 45% power.)
Gross weight . . . . 3600 pounds
Empty weight (includes standard avionics) . . . . 2191 pounds
Useful load . . . . 1421 pounds

Stall speed (landing, full flaps) . . . . 60 MPH
Rate of climb at sea level . . . . 1030 feet per minute
Service ceiling . . . . 16,600 feet

Airspeed limits   Maneuvering . . . . 160 MPH
                  Maximum structural cruising . . . . 190 MPH
                  Never exceed . . . . 234 MPH
                  Flaps extended (normal) . . . . 140 MPH
                  Landing gear extended (normal) . . . . 175 MPH
Fuel . . . . 100/130 octane minimum

The 1980 A36 Bonanza had a new exterior paint design. The interior remained the same as the 1979 model. Serial numbers were E-1594 through E-1765 . . . a total of 172 units. The Power Plant was the Continental IO-520-BB rated at 285 H.P. The 1980 standard equipped price was $99,250.

THESE CHANGES OCCURRED DURING PRODUCTION:

- Reduced aileron freeplay, E-1722 and after,
- Power supply bracket change, E-1638 and after
- New voltage regulator, E-1644 and after,
- Landing gear motor change, E-1626 and after,
- Airspeed indicator with approach flap white triangle, E-1594 and after,
- Static system test point, E-1610 and after,
- External power relay control, E-1618 and after,
- 1980 noise level reduction, E-1609 and after,
- 80 gallon fuel system as standard equipment, E-1594 and after,
- Longer control column assembly to protect radios, E-1719 and after,
- Turn coordinator with power warning indication, E-1647 unlighted, E-1662 lighted,
- Openable window latch revision, E-1751 and after,
- Quick release fastener — oxygen bottle door. E-1727 and after,
- Hartzell propeller, E-1716 and after,
- Narco ELT installation, E-1687 and after.

A36

BONANZA

MODEL YEAR 1981

Top speed at sea level.................................... 206 MPH
Maximum recommended cruise power .... 75% (214 HP)
Cruise speed at 75% power at 6000 feet (optimum altitude)
    full throttle, 2500 RPM............................... 193 MPH
Standard fuel capacity.................................... 74 gallons
Maximum range (at 167 MPH at 10,000 feet)
    with standard tanks.................................. 861 miles
(Range includes allowance for warm-up, taxi, takeoff, climb,
      and a 45-minute reserve at 45% power.)
Gross weight .... 3600 pounds
Empty weight (includes standard avionics) .... 2195 pounds
Useful load .... 1417 pounds

Stall speed (landing, full flaps) .... 60 MPH
Rate of climb at sea level .... 1030 feet per minute
Service ceiling .... 16,600 feet

Airspeed limits   Maneuvering .... 160 MPH
                 Maximum structural cruising............... 190 MPH
                 Never exceed........................... 234 MPH
                 Flaps extended (normal) .... 140 MPH
                 Landing gear extended (normal) .... 175 MPH
Fuel.................................... 100/130 octane minimum

The 1981 A36 Bonanza had the same interior and the same exterior paint design as the 1980 model. Serial numbers were E-1766 through E-1931 . . . 166 units. The Power Plant was the Continental IO-520-BB rated at 285 H.P. The 1981 standard equipped price was $115,000.

THESE CHANGES OCCURRED DURING PRODUCTION:

- Windshield retainer and sealant change, E-1840 and after,
- Improved engine control cable, E-1799 and after,
- Starter energized annunciator light, E-1766 and after,
- Knots only airspeed standard, E-1766 and after,
- Fresh air blower, E-1809 and after,
- Elevator trim system improvement, E-1857 and after,
- Aerosonic fuel flow system, E-1766 and after,
- Fire extinguisher relocation, E-1766 and after,
- Elevator weight change, E-1782 and after,
- Elevator cable guard, E-1816 and after,
- Landing gear actuator assembly with slower speed motor, E-1876 and after,
- Copilot seat back restraint, E-1778 and after,
- Improved corrosion protection (wing attach bolts), E-1847 and after,
- Cabin fresh air blower, E-1809 and after,
- Elevator trim system improvement, E-1857 and after,
- New engine winter baffles, E-1766 and after,
- Improved dynamic brake relay, E-1906 and after.

A36

BONANZA   MODEL YEAR 1982

Top speed at sea level.................................... 206 MPH
Maximum recommended cruise power.................. 75% (214 HP)
Cruise speed at 75% power at 6000 feet (optimum altitude)
    full throttle, 2500 RPM............................... 193 MPH
Standard fuel capacity..................................... 74 gallons
Maximum range (at 167 MPH at 10,000 feet)
    with standard tanks................................. 861 miles
(Range includes allowance for warm-up, taxi, takeoff, climb,
    and a 45-minute reserve at 45% power.)
Gross weight .... 3600 pounds
Empty weight (includes standard avionics) .... 2195 pounds
Useful load .... 1417 pounds

Stall speed (landing, full flaps) ....60 MPH
Rate of climb at sea level .... 1030 feet per minute
Service ceiling .... 16,600 feet

Airspeed limits Maneuvering .... 160 MPH
              Maximum structural cruising............... 190 MPH
              Never exceed........................... 234 MPH
              Flaps extended (normal) .... 140 MPH
              Landing gear extended (normal) .... 175 MPH
Fuel.................................... 100/130 octane minimum

The 1982 A36 Bonanza had the same interior and the same exterior paint design as the 1981 model. This was the 50th anniversary of Beech Aircraft Corporation, so a special, officially designated medallion appears on the instrument panel of these airplanes. Serial numbers were E-1932 through E-2049 . . . 118 units. The Power Plant was the Continental IO-520-BB rated at 285 H.P. The 1982 standard equipped price was $126,650.

THESE CHANGES OCCURRED DURING PRODUCTION:

- New static wick installation, E-1932 and after,
- Openable window latch mechanism improvement, E-1960 and after,
- Optional three blade McCauley propeller, E-1932 and after,
- Standard aircraft corrosion proofing, E-1932 and after,
- Propeller de-ice installation, E-2042 and after,
- Improved alternator voltage regulator, E-2000 and after,
- External guide for hold open rod, E-2003 and after.

A36
BONANZA

Top speed at sea level.................................... 206 MPH
Maximum recommended cruise power .... 75% (214 HP)
Cruise speed at 75% power at 6000 feet (optimum altitude)
    full throttle, 2500 RPM.............................. 193 MPH
Standard fuel capacity..................................... 74 gallons
Maximum range (at 167 MPH at 10,000 feet)
    with standard tanks................................... 861 miles
(Range includes allowance for warm-up, taxi, takeoff, climb,
    and a 45-minute reserve at 45% power.)
Gross weight .... 3600 pounds
Empty weight (includes standard avionics) .... 2195 pounds
Useful load .... 1417 pounds

Stall speed (landing, full flaps) .... 60 MPH
Rate of climb at sea level .... 1030 feet per minute
Service ceiling .... 16,600 feet

Airspeed limits   Maneuvering .... 160 MPH
                     Maximum structural cruising............... 190 MPH
                     Never exceed........................... 234 MPH
                     Flaps extended (normal) .... 140 MPH
                     Landing gear extended (normal) .... 175 MPH
Fuel.................................... 100/130 octane minimum

The 1983 A36 Bonanza had the same interior and the same exterior paint design as the 1982 model. Serial numbers were E-2050 through E-2103, E-2105 through E-2110 . . . a total of 59 units. The Power Plant was the Continental IO-520-BB rated at 285 H.P. The 1983 standard equipped price was $142,500.

THESE CHANGES OCCURRED DURING PRODUCTION:

- Improved elevator push rods, E-2104, E-2106 and after,
- Fuel selector valve lockout device, E-2062 and after,
- Improved TCM compressor drive kit, E-2055 and after.

A36
BONANZA

MODEL YEAR 1984

Top speed at sea level.................................... 212 MPH
Maximum recommended cruise power .... 75% (214 HP)
Cruise speed at 75% power at 6000 feet (optimum altitude)
    full throttle, 2500 RPM........20° c Rich of Peak........ 202 MPH
Standard fuel capacity..................................... 74 gallons
Maximum range (at 167 MPH at 10,000 feet)
    with standard tanks..........20° c Rich of Peak......... 861 miles
(Range includes allowance for warm-up, taxi, takeoff, climb,
     and a 45-minute reserve at 45% power.)
Gross weight .... 3650 pounds
Empty weight (includes standard avionics) .... 2247 pounds
Useful load .... 1416 pounds

Stall speed (landing, full flaps) ....68 MPH
Rate of climb at sea level .... 1210 feet per minute
Service ceiling ....18,500 feet

Airspeed limits Maneuvering .... 160 MPH
                 Maximum structural cruising............... 190 MPH
                 Never exceed........................... 234 MPH
                 Flaps extended (normal) .... 140 MPH
                 Landing gear extended (normal) .... 175 MPH
Fuel.....................................100/130 octane minimum

New 1984 A36 Bonanza instrument panel

The 1984 A36 Bonanza featured the same interior and exterior paint design as the 1983 model. It had an all new instrument panel with new engine gages. It was also the first Bonanza to have individual pilot and copilot control columns. The leading edge wing vortex generators (originally developed for the F33C) greatly improved stall characteristics. Serial numbers were E-2104, E-2111 through E-2204 . . . a total of 95 units. The Power Plant was the new Continental IO-550-B rated at 300 H.P. The 1984 standard equipped price was $160,700.

THESE CHANGES OCCURRED DURING PRODUCTION:

- Air conditioner time delay relay, E-2104, E-2111 and after,
- Headliner material change, E-2116 and after,
- New overhead console with close focus reading lights, E-2104, E-2111 and after,
- New improved inertia reels, E-2091,
- Step and courtesy light timer, E-2111 and after,
- Improved static wick installation, E-2135 and after,
- Avionics ground communications switch, E-2104, E-2111 and after,
- Standard external power receptacle, E-2111 and after,

- Optional standby instrument air pressure pump, E-2180 and after,
- Airline type Scott Aviation oxygen masks, E-2104, E-2111 and after,
- Standby generator disconnect, E-2060 and after,
- Optional refreshment cabinet, E-2069 and after,
- Reduction of closing forces on utility doors, E-2180 and after,
- Electronic warning horn, E-2104, E-2111 and after,
- New rudder trim tab, E-2104 and after,
- Vertical adjusting pilot's seat, E-2104, E-2111 and after,
- Dorne and Margolin ELT installation, E-2148 and after,
- Vertical adjusting copilot's seat, E-2104, E-2111 and after,
- T-handle push/pull controls, E-2191 and after.

A36

BONANZA

MODEL YEAR 1985

Top speed at sea level................................... 212 MPH
Maximum recommended cruise power................. 75% (214 HP)
Cruise speed at 75% power at 6000 feet (optimum altitude)
      full throttle, 2500 RPM........ 20°c Rich of Peak........ 202 MPH
Standard fuel capacity.................................... 74 gallons
Maximum range (at 167 MPH at 10,000 feet)
      with standard tanks.......... 20°c Rich of Peak......... 861 miles
(Range includes allowance for warm-up, taxi, takeoff, climb,
      and a 45-minute reserve at 45% power.)
Gross weight .... 3650 pounds
Empty weight (includes standard avionics) .... 2247 pounds
Useful load .... 1416 pounds

Stall speed (landing, full flaps) .... 68 MPH
Rate of climb at sea level .... 1210 feet per minute
Service ceiling .... 18,500 feet

Airspeed limits   Maneuvering .... 160 MPH
                      Maximum structural cruising............... 190 MPH
                      Never exceed........................... 234 MPH
                      Flaps extended (normal) .... 140 MPH
                      Landing gear extended (normal) .... 175 MPH
Fuel.................................... 100/130 octane minimum

The 1985 A36 Bonanza featured the same interior and exterior paint design as the 1984 model. Serial numbers were E-2205 through E-2277, E-2279 through E-2289, and E-2293 through E-2295 . . . a total of 87 units. The Power Plant was the Continental IO-550-B rated at 300 H.P. The 1985 standard equipped price was $189,500.

THESE CHANGES OCCURRED DURING PRODUCTION:

- New flight hour meter, E-2234 and after,
- New winter baffles, E-2249 and after,
- Reduced diameter fuel cap adapters, E-2217 and after,
- Improved engine manifold fuel drain, E-2263 and after,
- Standby air pressure pump became standard equipment, E-2217 and after.

A36
BONANZA

MODEL YEAR 1986

Top speed at sea level. . . . . 212 MPH
Maximum recommended cruise power . . . . 75% (214 HP)
Cruise speed at 75% power at 6000 feet (optimum altitude)
    full throttle, 2500 RPM. . . . . . . 20° c Rich of Peak. . . . . 202 MPH
Standard fuel capacity. . . . . 74 gallons
Maximum range (at 167 MPH at 10,000 feet)
    with standard tanks. . . . . 20° c Rich of Peak. . . . . 861 miles
(Range includes allowance for warm-up, taxi, takeoff, climb,
    and a 45-minute reserve at 45% power.)
Gross weight . . . . 3650 pounds
Empty weight (includes standard avionics) . . . . 2278 pounds
Useful load . . . . 1385 pounds

Stall speed (landing, full flaps) . . . . 68 MPH
Rate of climb at sea level . . . . 1210 feet per minute
Service ceiling . . . . 18,500 feet

Airspeed limits Maneuvering . . . . 160 MPH
                    Maximum structural cruising. . . . . 190 MPH
                    Never exceed. . . . . 234 MPH
                    Flaps extended (normal) . . . . 140 MPH
                    Landing gear extended (normal) . . . . 175 MPH
Fuel. . . . . 100/130 octane minimum

The 1986 A36 Bonanza had the same interior and exterior paint design as the 1985 model.

Serial numbers were E-2278, E-2290, E-2291, E-2292, E-2296 through E-2352 . . . a total of 61 units. The Power Plant was the Continental IO-550-B rated at 300 H.P. The 1986 standard equipped price was $197,275.

THESE CHANGES OCCURRED DURING PRODUCTION:

- Tachometer driven by an electric transducer, E-2340 and after,
- Flap and landing gear switch knob change, E-2349 and after,
- Change to Slick magnetoes, E-2318 and after.

A36

BONANZA

MODEL YEAR 1987

Top speed at sea level................................... 212 MPH
Maximum recommended cruise power .... 75% (214 HP)
Cruise speed at 75% power at 6000 feet (optimum altitude)
    full throttle, 2500 RPM........20° c Rich of Peak........ 202 MPH
Standard fuel capacity..................................... 74 gallons
Maximum range (at 167 MPH at 10,000 feet)
    with standard tanks..........20° c Rich of Peak......... 861 miles
(Range includes allowance for warm-up, taxi, takeoff, climb,
    and a 45-minute reserve at 45% power.)
Gross weight .... 3650 pounds
Empty weight (includes standard avionics) .... 2278 pounds
Useful load .... 1385 pounds

Stall speed (landing, full flaps) ....68 MPH
Rate of climb at sea level .... 1210 feet per minute
Service ceiling .... 18,500 feet

Airspeed limits Maneuvering .... 160 MPH
               Maximum structural cruising................ 190 MPH
               Never exceed........................... 234 MPH
               Flaps extended (normal) .... 140 MPH
               Landing gear extended (normal) .... 175 MPH
Fuel..................................... 100/130 octane minimum

The 1987 A36 Bonanza had the same interior and exterior paint design as the 1986 model. Serial numbers were E-2353 through E-2402 . . . a total of 50 units. The Power Plant was the Continental IO-550-B rated at 300 H.P. The 1987 standard equipped price was $207,150.

THESE CHANGES OCCURRED DURING PRODUCTION:

- Firewall insulation change, E-2372, E-2377 and after,
- New voltage regulator, E-2374 and after,
- Inlet duct improvement, E-2391 and after,
- Improved window seal, E-2368 and after,
- Standby instrument air system pressure switch change, E-2368 and after,
- Model identification plate relocation, E-2400 and after.

A36

BONANZA

MODEL YEAR 1988

Top speed at sea level . . . . 212 MPH
Maximum recommended cruise power . . . . 75% (214 HP)
Cruise speed at 75% power at 6000 feet (optimum altitude)
    full throttle, 2500 RPM . . . . 20° c Rich of Peak . . . . 202 MPH
Standard fuel capacity . . . . 74 gallons
Maximum range (at 167 MPH at 10,000 feet)
    with standard tanks . . . . 20° c Rich of Peak . . . . 861 miles
(Range includes allowance for warm-up, taxi, takeoff, climb,
       and a 45-minute reserve at 45% power.)
Gross weight . . . . 3650 pounds
Empty weight (includes standard avionics) . . . . 2266 pounds
Useful load . . . . 1397 pounds

Stall speed (landing, full flaps) . . . . 68 MPH
Rate of climb at sea level . . . . 1208 feet per minute
Service ceiling . . . . 18,500 feet

Airspeed limits Maneuvering . . . . 160 MPH
                Maximum structural cruising . . . . 190 MPH
                Never exceed . . . . 234 MPH
                Flaps extended (normal) . . . . 140 MPH
                Landing gear extended (normal) . . . . 175 MPH
Fuel . . . . 100/130 octane minimum

The 1988 A36 Bonanza had the same interior and exterior paint design as the 1987 model. Serial numbers were E-2403 through E-2467 . . . 65 units. The Power Plant was the Continental IO-550-B rated at 300 H.P. The 1988 standard equipped price was $217,500.

THESE CHANGES OCCURRED DURING PRODUCTION:

- Fuel boost pump vane improvement, E-2420 and after,
- Change to narco ELT, E-2424 and after,
- Electronic warning horn change, E-2465 and after,
- Removal of sound deadener from firewall and adjacent skins, E-2406, E-2410 and after.

A36
BONANZA

MODEL YEAR 1989

Top speed at sea level.................................... 212 MPH
Maximum recommended cruise power ....75% (214 HP)
Cruise speed at 75% power at 6000 feet (optimum altitude)
    full throttle, 2500 RPM........20° c Rich of Peak........ 202 MPH
Standard fuel capacity...................................74 gallons
Maximum range (at 167 MPH at 10,000 feet)
    with standard tanks..........20° c Rich of Peak......... 861 miles
(Range includes allowance for warm-up, taxi, takeoff, climb,
    and a 45-minute reserve at 45% power.)
Gross weight .... 3650 pounds
Empty weight (includes standard avionics) .... 2266 pounds
Useful load .... 1397 pounds

Stall speed (landing, full flaps) ....68 MPH
Rate of climb at sea level .... 1208 feet per minute
Service ceiling .... 18,500 feet

Airspeed limits   Maneuvering .... 160 MPH
                      Maximum structural cruising............... 190 MPH
                      Never exceed........................... 234 MPH
                      Flaps extended (normal) .... 140 MPH
                      Landing gear extended (normal) .... 175 MPH
Fuel....................................100/130 octane minimum

The 1989 A36 Bonanza had the same interior and exterior paint design as the 1988 model. Serial numbers were E-2468 through E-2518 . . . a total of 51 units. The Power Plant was the Continental IO-550-B rated at 300 H.P. The 1989 standard equipped price was $235,400.

THIS CHANGE OCCURRED DURING PRODUCTION:

- Cowl assembly skin thickness change, E-2496 and after.

A36

BONANZA

MODEL YEAR 1990

Top speed at sea level.................................. 212 MPH
Maximum recommended cruise power .... 75% (214 HP)
Cruise speed at 75% power at 6000 feet (optimum altitude)
    full throttle, 2500 RPM........20° c Rich of Peak........ 202 MPH
Standard fuel capacity..................................... 74 gallons
Maximum range (at 167 MPH at 10,000 feet)
    with standard tanks..........20° c Rich of Peak......... 861 miles
(Range includes allowance for warm-up, taxi, takeoff, climb,
    and a 45-minute reserve at 45% power.)
Gross weight .... 3650 pounds
Empty weight (includes standard avionics) .... 2266 pounds
Useful load .... 1397 pounds

Stall speed (landing, full flaps) .... 68 MPH
Rate of climb at sea level .... 1208 feet per minute
Service ceiling .... 18,500 feet

Airspeed limits Maneuvering .... 160 MPH
                  Maximum structural cruising................ 190 MPH
                  Never exceed............................ 234 MPH
                  Flaps extended (normal) .... 140 MPH
                  Landing gear extended (normal) .... 175 MPH
Fuel.................................... 100/130 octane minimum

The 1990 A36 Bonanza had the same interior and exterior paint design as the 1989 model. Serial numbers began with E-2519 and ended with E-2586 . . . a total of 68 units. The Power Plant was the Continental IO-550-B rated at 300 H.P. The 1990 standard equipped price was $257,500.

THIS CHANGE OCCURRED DURING PRODUCTION:

- Air conditioner time delay relay change, E-2540 and after.

A36-TC

BONANZA   **MODEL YEAR 1979**

Performance with the turbocharged TSIO-520-UB:

Top speed at 19,000 feet . . . . 246 MPH
Maximum recommended cruise power . . . . 79% (237 HP)
Cruise speed at 79% power at 25,000 feet
    full throttle, 2500 RPM. . . . . 229 MPH
Standard fuel capacity. . . . . 74 gallons
Maximum range (at 196 MPH at 25,000 feet)
    with standard tanks. . . . . 840 miles
   (Range includes allowance for warm-up, taxi, takeoff, climb
       and a 45-minute reserve at 45% power.)
Gross weight . . . . 3650 pounds
Empty weight (includes standard avionics) . . . . 2269 pounds
Useful load . . . . 1397 pounds

Stall speed (landing, full flaps) . . . . .66 MPH
Rate of climb at sea level . . . . 1165 feet per minute
Service ceiling . . . . above 25,000 feet

Maximum altitude limitation. . . . . .25,000 feet
Airspeed limits   Maneuvering . . . . 160 MPH
                Maximum structural cruising. . . . . 190 MPH
                Never exceed. . . . . 234 MPH
                Flaps extended (normal) . . . . 142 MPH
                Landing gear extended (normal) . . . . 175 MPH
Fuel. . . . . 100/130 octane minimum

Beechcraft Bonanza A36-TC — 1979.

The 1979 A36-TC Bonanza was the first turbocharged Bonanza since the 1970 V35B-TC. Serial numbers are EA-1 through EA-32. The Power Plant was the Continental TSIO-520-UB rated at 300 H.P. The 1979 standard equipped price was $98,800. The word TURBO (in the picture) was not used on the tail. There was a fear the airplane might be fueled with turbine fuel.

THESE CHANGES OCCURRED DURING PRODUCTION:

- New seals for openable windows, EA-1 and after,
- Dual brakes shuttle valve change, EA-1 and after,
- Torque adjusting sunvisor, EA-15 and after,
- 28-volt propeller de-icing, EA-2 and after,
- Oxygen bottle installation, EA-2 and after,
- Duct installation — cabin air exhaust drain, EA-8 and after,
- Approach flap position on flap switch, EA-1 and after,
- 1979 interior change, EA-3 and after,
- Emergency exit placard improvement, EA-3 and after,
- New emergency locator transmitter, EA-3 and after,
- TCM 100 AMP alternator, EA-6 and after,

- Landing gear limit switch adjustment, EA-3 and after,
- Series plumbing for dual brakes, EA-3 and after,
- Louver installation change, EA-3 and after,
- Floating panel bonding strap, EA-5 and after,
- Improved openable window sealing, EA-3 and after,
- Radar antenna installation, EA-11 and after,
- Liquid crystal digital clock, EA-6 and after,
- Waste gate drain tube improvement, EA-13 and after,
- Lower rotating beacon connector addition, EA-12 and after,
- Heat shield support bracket, EA-15 and after,
- Openable window latch improvement, EA-21, EA-28,
- Flight with utility doors removed, EA-1 and after,
- Temperature improved liquid crystal digital clock, EA-26 and after.

A36-TC

BONANZA

MODEL YEAR 1980

Performance with the turbocharged TSIO-520-UB:

Top speed at 19,000 feet .... 246 MPH
Maximum recommended cruise power .... 79% (237 HP)
Cruise speed at 79% power at 25,000 feet
     full throttle, 2500 RPM .... 229 MPH
Standard fuel capacity .... 74 gallons
Maximum range (at 196 MPH at 25,000 feet)
     with standard tanks .... 840 miles
    (Range includes allowance for warm-up, taxi, takeoff, climb
        and a 45-minute reserve at 45% power.)
Gross weight .... 3650 pounds
Empty weight (includes standard avionics) .... 2269 pounds
Useful load .... 1397 pounds

Stall speed (landing, full flaps) .... 66 MPH
Rate of climb at sea level .... 1165 feet per minute
Service ceiling .... above 25,000 feet

Maximum altitude limitation .... 25,000 feet
Airspeed limits   Maneuvering .... 160 MPH
               Maximum structural cruising .... 190 MPH
               Never exceed .... 234 MPH
               Flaps extended (normal) .... 142 MPH
               Landing gear extended (normal) .... 175 MPH
Fuel .... 100/130 octane minimum

The 1980 A36-TC had a new interior but the same exterior paint design as the 1979 model. Serial numbers were EA-33 through EA-158... 126 units. The Power Plant was the Continental TSIO-520-UB rated at 300 H.P. The 1980 standard equipped price was $111,250.

THESE CHANGES OCCURRED DURING PRODUCTION:

- Power supply bracket change, EA-60 and after,
- New voltage regulator, EA-58 and after,
- New one piece doubler in left hand nose skin, EA-88 and after,
- Reduced aileron freeplay, EA-108 and after,
- Landing gear motor change, EA-49 and after,
- Static system test point, EA-42 and after,
- External power relay control, EA-46 and after,
- Standby generator installation, EA-52 and after,
- 80 gallon fuel system as standard equipment, EA-33 and after,
- Openable window latch improvement, EA-33 and after,
- Longer control column assembly to protect radios, EA-105 and after,
- Turn coordinator with power warning indicator, unlighted EA-68 and after, lighted EA-70 and after,
- Throttle cable support, EA-35, EA-39 and after,
- Quick release fastener — oxygen bottle door, EA-116 and after,
- Narco ELT installation, EA-81 and after,
- Fire extinguisher relocation, EA-33, EA-100,
- Hartzell propeller, EA-106 through EA-109. EA-111 through EA-117, EA-119 and after,
- Induction tube drain hole, EA-90 and after.

A36-TC

BONANZA   **MODEL YEAR 1981**

Performance with the turbocharged TSIO-520-UB:

Top speed at 19,000 feet .... 246 MPH
Maximum recommended cruise power .... 79% (237 HP)
Cruise speed at 79% power at 25,000 feet
    full throttle, 2500 RPM............................. 229 MPH
Standard fuel capacity..................................... 74 gallons
Maximum range (at 196 MPH at 25,000 feet)
    with standard tanks.................................. 840 miles
   (Range includes allowance for warm-up, taxi, takeoff, climb
      and a 45-minute reserve at 45% power.)
Gross weight .... 3650 pounds
Empty weight (includes standard avionics) .... 2269 pounds
Useful load .... 1397 pounds

Stall speed (landing, full flaps) ....66 MPH
Rate of climb at sea level .... 1165 feet per minute
Service ceiling .... above 25,000 feet

Maximum altitude limitation .... 25,000 feet
Airspeed limits   Maneuvering .... 160 MPH
                 Maximum structural cruising............... 190 MPH
                 Never exceed........................... 234 MPH
                 Flaps extended (normal) .... 142 MPH
                 Landing gear extended (normal) .... 175 MPH
Fuel.................................... 100/130 octane minimum

The 1981 A36-TC Bonanza had the same interior and exterior paint design as the 1980 model. Serial numbers are EA-159 through EA-241, and EA-243 through EA-272 . . . a total of 113 units. The Power Plant was the Continental TSIO-520-UB rated at 300 H.P. The 1981 standard equipped price was $129,000.

THESE CHANGES OCCURRED DURING PRODUCTION:

- Aerosonic fuel flow system, EA-159 and after,
- Fire extinguisher relocation, EA-159 and after,
- Elevator weight change, EA-170 and after,
- Elevator cable guard, EA-197 and after,
- Landing gear actuator assembly with slower speed motor, EA-239 and after,
- Copilot seat back restraint, EA-168 and after,
- Improved corrosion protection (wing attach bolts) EA-221 and after,
- Cabin fresh air blower, EA-192 and after,
- Engine air reference hose change, EA-165,
- Elevator trim system improvement, EA-227 and after,
- Turbocharger oil return system, EA-243 and after,
- Improved fuel supply system, EA-242,
- Improved dynamic brake relay, EA-254 and after.

B36-TC

BONANZA

Performance with the turbocharged TSIO-520-UB:

Top speed at 19,000 feet .... 245 MPH
Maximum recommended cruise power .... 79% (237 HP)
Cruise speed at 79% power at 25,000 feet
    full throttle, 2500 RPM............................... 230 MPH
Standard fuel capacity............ 108 gallons total, usable is 102 gallons
Maximum range (at 196 MPH at 25,000 feet)
    with standard tanks................................. 1133 miles
(Range includes allowance for warm-up, taxi, takeoff, climb
    and a 45-minute reserve at 45% power.)
Gross weight .... 3850 pounds
Empty weight (includes standard avionics) .... 2338 pounds
Useful load .... 1528 pounds

Stall speed (landing, full flaps) ....66 MPH
Rate of climb at sea level .... 1049 feet per minute
Service ceiling .... above 25,000 feet

Maximum altitude limitation............................ 25,000 feet
Airspeed limits   Maneuvering .... 162 MPH
                Maximum structural cruising............... 193 MPH
                Never exceed........................... 237 MPH
                Flaps extended (normal) .... 144 MPH
                Landing gear extended (normal) .... 177 MPH
Fuel .... 100/130 octane minimum

The 1981 B36-TC was the prototype for the 1982 B36-TC Bonanza. The serial number is EA-242 . . . one unit only. The Power Plant was the Continental TSIO-520-UB rated at 300 H.P. The 1981 standard equipped price was $129,000.

B36-TC

BONANZA

MODEL YEAR 1982

Performance with the turbocharged TSIO-520-UB:

Top speed at 19,000 feet . . . . 245 MPH
Maximum recommended cruise power . . . . 79% (237 HP)
Cruise speed at 79% power at 25,000 feet
     full throttle, 2500 RPM . . . . 230 MPH
Standard fuel capacity . . . . 108 gallons total, usable is 102 gallons
Maximum range (at 196 MPH at 25,000 feet)
     with standard tanks . . . . 1133 miles
(Range includes allowance for warm-up, taxi, takeoff, climb
     and a 45-minute reserve at 45% power.)
Gross weight . . . . 3850 pounds
Empty weight (includes standard avionics) . . . . 2338 pounds
Useful load . . . . 1528 pounds

Stall speed (landing, full flaps) . . . . 66 MPH
Rate of climb at sea level . . . . 1049 feet per minute
Service ceiling . . . . above 25,000 feet

Maximum altitude limitation . . . . 25,000 feet
Airspeed limits Maneuvering . . . . 162 MPH
                   Maximum structural cruising . . . . 193 MPH
                   Never exceed . . . . 237 MPH
                   Flaps extended (normal) . . . . 144 MPH
                   Landing gear extended (normal) . . . . 177 MPH
Fuel . . . . 100/130 octane minimum

The 1982 B36-TC Bonanza had the same interior and exterior paint design as the 1981 model. This was the 50th anniversary of Beech Aircraft Corporation. So a special, officially designated medallion appears on the instrument panel of these airplanes. Serial numbers are EA-273 through EA-319, EA-321 through EA-323 . . . a total of 51 units. All the B36-TC's had baron wing tips for an increase in wing span of four feet, four inches. This was done to offset the effect of the higher gross weight on climb performance. The Power Plant was the Continental TSIO-520-UB rated at 300 H.P. The 1982 standard equipped price was $151,350.

THESE CHANGES OCCURRED DURING PRODUCTION:

- Whelen rotating beacon, EA-288 and after,
- Landing gear switch guard installation, EA-273 and after,
- New static wick installation, EA-273 and after,
- New openable window latch mechanism, EA-273 and after,
- New instrument panel, EA-320 and after,
- Landing gear safety system relay installation, EA-256 and after,
- Throttle body shield assembly improvement, EA-242, EA-273 and after,
- Standard aircraft corrosion proofing, EA-273 and after,
- Improved fuel supply system, EA-273 and after,
- Propeller de-icing installation, EA-309, and after,
- External guide for hold open rod, EA-218 through EA-314, EA-318 and after,
- Improved alternator voltage regulator, EA-278 and after,
- New optional streamlined belly beacon, EA-320 and after,
- Common landing gear actuator, EA-306, EA-320 and after,
- Avionics coupler installation change, EA-273 and after,
- Aileron control cable link change, EA-273 and after.

B36-TC

BONANZA   **MODEL YEAR 1983**

Performance with the turbocharged TSIO-520-UB:

Top speed at 19,000 feet .... 245 MPH
Maximum recommended cruise power .... 79% (237 HP)
Cruise speed at 79% power at 25,000 feet
    full throttle, 2500 RPM.............................. 230 MPH
Standard fuel capacity....... 108 gallons total, usable is ...... 102 gallons
Maximum range (at 196 MPH at 25,000 feet)
    with standard tanks................................ 1133 miles
    (Range includes allowance for warm-up, taxi, takeoff, climb
        and a 45-minute reserve at 45% power.)
Gross weight .... 3850 pounds
Empty weight (includes standard avionics) .... 2338 pounds
Useful load .... 1528 pounds

Stall speed (landing, full flaps) ....66 MPH
Rate of climb at sea level .... 1049 feet per minute
Service ceiling .... above 25,000 feet

Maximum altitude limitation ....25,000 feet
Airspeed limits   Maneuvering .... 162 MPH
                Maximum structural cruising................ 193 MPH
                Never exceed............................ 237 MPH
                Flaps extended (normal) .... 144 MPH
                Landing gear extended (normal) .... 177 MPH
Fuel.................................... 100/130 octane minimum

The 1983 B36-TC Bonanza had the same interior but an all new exterior paint design. Serial numbers were EA-324 through EA-388 . . . a total of 65 units. The Power Plant was the Continental TSIO-520-UB rated at 300 H.P. The standard equipped price in 1983 was $164,000.

THESE CHANGES OCCURRED DURING PRODUCTION:

- Common landing gear actuator, EA-342 and after,
- New optional streamlined belly beacon, EA-327 and after,
- Optional refreshment cabinet, EA-328, EA-343 and after,
- Standby generator disconnect, E-334 and after,
- Alternator auxiliary fuse, E-324 and after,
- New rudder trim tab, EA-383 and after.

B36-TC

BONANZA

MODEL YEAR 1984

Performance with the turbocharged TSIO-520-UB:

Top speed at 19,000 feet . . . . 245 MPH

Maximum recommended cruise power . . . . 79% (237 HP)

Cruise speed at 79% power at 25,000 feet
   full throttle, 2500 RPM . . . . 230 MPH

Standard fuel capacity . . . . 108 gallons total, usable is 102 gallons

Maximum range (at 196 MPH at 25,000 feet)
   with standard tanks . . . . 1133 miles

(Range includes allowance for warm-up, taxi, takeoff, climb
      and a 45-minute reserve at 45% power.)

Gross weight . . . . 3850 pounds

Empty weight (includes standard avionics) . . . . 2338 pounds

Useful load . . . . 1528 pounds

Stall speed (landing, full flaps) . . . . 66 MPH

Rate of climb at sea level . . . . 1049 feet per minute

Service ceiling . . . . above 25,000 feet

Maximum altitude limitation . . . . 25,000 feet

Airspeed limits Maneuvering . . . . 162 MPH

                Maximum structural cruising . . . . 193 MPH

                Never exceed . . . . 237 MPH

                Flaps extended (normal) . . . . 144 MPH

                Landing gear extended (normal) . . . . 177 MPH

Fuel . . . . 100/130 octane minimum

The 1984 B36-TC Bonanza had the same interior and exterior paint design as the 1983 model. It had an all new instrument panel with new engine gages. It was also, along with the 1984 A36, the first Bonanza to have individual pilot and copilot control columns. The leading edge wing vortex generators (originally developed for the F33C) greatly improved stall characteristics. Serial numbers were EA-320, E-389 through EA-442 . . . 54 units. The Power Plant was the Continental TSIO-520-UB rated at 300 H.P. The standard equipped price in 1984 was $182,100.

THESE CHANGES OCCURRED DURING PRODUCTION:

- Electronic warning horn, EA-389 and after,
- Reduction of closing forces on the utility doors, EA-434 and after,
- New overhead console with close focus reading lights, EA-320,
- New inertia reels, EA-320 and after,
- Step and courtesy light timer, EA-320 and after,
- Avionics ground communications switch, EA-320 and after,
- Airline type Scott Aviation oxygen mask, EA-320 and after,
- Alternator auxiliary fuse, EA-320 and after,
- Electronic warning horn, EA-320 and after,
- Vertical adjusting pilot's seat, EA-320, EA-389 and after,
- Vertical adjusting copilot's seat, EA-320, EA-389 and after,
- Track seat support change, EA-320, EA-389 and after,
- New alternator, EA-320, EA-389 and after,
- New rudder trim tab, E-383 and after,
- Oxygen manifold face plate change, EA-414 and after,
- Dorne and Margolin ELT installation, EA-412 and after,
- New engine starter, EA-395 and after,
- T-handle push/pull controls, EA-441 and after,
- Standby generator isolation diode, EA-411 and after,
- Pressurized Slick magnetos, EA-440 and after,
- Improved turbocharger outlet check valve, EA-383, EA-397, EA-405, EA-410, EA-416, EA-417, EA-419 and after,
- New overhead console with close focus reading lights, EA-389 and after,
- Optional standby instrument air pump, EA-422 and after.

B36-TC

BONANZA

Performance with the turbocharged TSIO-520-UB:

Top speed at 19,000 feet .... 245 MPH
Maximum recommended cruise power .... 79% (237 HP)
Cruise speed at 79% power at 25,000 feet
    full throttle, 2500 RPM............................... 230 MPH
Standard fuel capacity............ 108 gallons total, usable is 102 gallons
Maximum range (at 196 MPH at 25,000 feet)
    with standard tanks................................. 1133 miles
    (Range includes allowance for warm-up, taxi, takeoff, climb
        and a 45-minute reserve at 45% power.)
Gross weight .... 3850 pounds
Empty weight (includes standard avionics) .... 2338 pounds
Useful load .... 1528 pounds

Stall speed (landing, full flaps) ....66 MPH
Rate of climb at sea level .... 1049 feet per minute
Service ceiling .... above 25,000 feet

Maximum altitude limitation .... 25,000 feet
Airspeed limits   Maneuvering .... 162 MPH
               Maximum structural cruising................ 193 MPH
               Never exceed............................ 237 MPH
               Flaps extended (normal) .... 144 MPH
               Landing gear extended (normal) .... 177 MPH
Fuel.................................... 100/130 octane minimum

The 1985 B36-TC Bonanza had the same interior and exterior paint design as the 1984 model. Serial numbers were EA-443 through EA-451 . . . only 8 units. The Power Plant was the Continental TSIO-520-UB rated at 300 H.P. The standard equipped price in 1985 was $213,500.

THESE CHANGES OCCURRED DURING PRODUCTION:

- Spar cover air conditioner installation improvement, EA-443 and after,
- Reduced diameter fuel cap adapters, E-448 and after,
- Standby air pressure pump as standard equipment, EA-443 and after.

B36-TC

BONANZA

Performance with the turbocharged TSIO-520-UB:

Top speed at 19,000 feet . . . . 245 MPH
Maximum recommended cruise power . . . . 79% (237 HP)
Cruise speed at 79% power at 25,000 feet
    full throttle, 2500 RPM . . . . 230 MPH
Standard fuel capacity . . . . 108 gallons total, usable is 102 gallons
Maximum range (at 196 MPH at 25,000 feet)
    with standard tanks . . . . 1133 miles
  (Range includes allowance for warm-up, taxi, takeoff, climb
      and a 45-minute reserve at 45% power.)
Gross weight . . . . 3850 pounds
Empty weight (includes standard avionics) . . . . 2338 pounds
Useful load . . . . 1528 pounds

Stall speed (landing, full flaps) . . . . 66 MPH
Rate of climb at sea level . . . . 1049 feet per minute
Service ceiling . . . . above 25,000 feet

Maximum altitude limitation . . . . 25,000 feet
Airspeed limits Maneuvering . . . . 162 MPH
                Maximum structural cruising . . . . 193 MPH
                Never exceed . . . . 237 MPH
                Flaps extended (normal) . . . . 144 MPH
                Landing gear extended (normal) . . . . 177 MPH
Fuel . . . . 100/130 octane minimum

The 1986 B36-TC Bonanza had the same interior as the 1985 model but a new exterior paint design. Serial numbers were EA-452 through EA-461 . . . 10 units. The Power Plant was the Continental TSIO-520-UB rated at 300 H.P. The standard equipped price in 1986 was $222,250.

THESE CHANGES OCCURRED DURING PRODUCTION:

- New seat actuator handle, EA-455 and after,
- Flap and landing gear switch knob change, EA-460 and after.

B36-TC

BONANZA **MODEL YEAR 1987**

Performance with the turbocharged TSIO-520-UB:

Top speed at 19,000 feet . . . . 245 MPH
Maximum recommended cruise power . . . . 79% (237 HP)
Cruise speed at 79% power at 25,000 feet
    full throttle, 2500 RPM . . . . 230 MPH
Standard fuel capacity . . . . 108 gallons total, usable is 102 gallons
Maximum range (at 196 MPH at 25,000 feet)
    with standard tanks . . . . 1133 miles
(Range includes allowance for warm-up, taxi, takeoff, climb
    and a 45-minute reserve at 45% power.)
Gross weight . . . . 3850 pounds
Empty weight (includes standard avionics) . . . . 2338 pounds
Useful load . . . . 1528 pounds

Stall speed (landing, full flaps) . . . . 66 MPH
Rate of climb at sea level . . . . 1049 feet per minute
Service ceiling . . . . above 25,000 feet

Maximum altitude limitation . . . . 25,000 feet
Airspeed limits   Maneuvering . . . . 162 MPH
                 Maximum structural cruising . . . . 193 MPH
                 Never exceed . . . . 237 MPH
                 Flaps extended (normal) . . . . 144 MPH
                 Landing gear extended (normal) . . . . 177 MPH
Fuel . . . . 100/130 octane minimum

The 1987 B36-TC Bonanza had the same interior and exterior paint design as the 1986 model. Serial numbers were EA-462 through EA-473 . . . 12 units. The Power Plant was the Continental TSIO-520-UB rated at 300 H.P. The standard equipped price in 1987 was $233,250.

THESE CHANGES OCCURRED DURING PRODUCTION:

- Firewall insulation change, EA-466 and after,
- Voltage regulator change, EA-466 and after,
- Model identification plate relocation, EA-473 and after,
- Standby instrument air system pressure switch change, EA-464 and after,
- Removal of sound deadner from firewall and adjacent skins, EA-471 and after,
- Front spar carry-thru web change, EA-472 and after,
- Improved window seal, EA-465 and after.

B36-TC

BONANZA

MODEL YEAR 1988

Performance with the turbocharged TSIO-520-UB:

Top speed at 19,000 feet .... 245 MPH
Maximum recommended cruise power .... 79% (237 HP)
Cruise speed at 79% power at 25,000 feet
     full throttle, 2500 RPM............................... 230 MPH
Standard fuel capacity .... 108 gallons total, usable is 102 gallons
Maximum range (at 196 MPH at 25,000 feet)
     with standard tanks .... 1133 miles
(Range includes allowance for warm-up, taxi, takeoff, climb
     and a 45-minute reserve at 45% power.)
Gross weight .... 3850 pounds
Empty weight (includes standard avionics) .... 2338 pounds
Useful load .... 1528 pounds

Stall speed (landing, full flaps) .... 66 MPH
Rate of climb at sea level .... 1049 feet per minute
Service ceiling .... above 25,000 feet

Maximum altitude limitation .... 25,000 feet
Airspeed limits Maneuvering .... 162 MPH
                  Maximum structural cruising................ 193 MPH
                  Never exceed .... 237 MPH
                  Flaps extended (normal) .... 144 MPH
                  Landing gear extended (normal) .... 177 MPH
Fuel .... 100/130 octane minimum

The 1988 B36-TC Bonanza had the same interior and exterior paint design as the 1987 model. Serial numbers were EA-474 through EA-488 . . . a total of 15 units. The Power Plant was the Continental TSIO-520-UB rated at 300 H.P. The standard equipped price in 1988 was $244,800.

THESE CHANGES OCCURRED DURING PRODUCTION:

- NARCO emergency locator transmitter, EA-480 and after,
- Removal of sound deadner from firewall and adjacent skins, EA-475 and after,
- Electronic warning horn change, EA-488 and after.

B36-TC

BONANZA   **MODEL YEAR 1989**

Performance with the turbocharged TSIO-520-UB:

Top speed at 19,000 feet . . . . 245 MPH
Maximum recommended cruise power . . . . 79% (237 HP)
Cruise speed at 79% power at 25,000 feet
     full throttle, 2500 RPM . . . . 230 MPH
Standard fuel capacity . . . . 108 gallons total, usable is 102 gallons
Maximum range (at 196 MPH at 25,000 feet)
     with standard tanks . . . . 1133 miles
     (Range includes allowance for warm-up, taxi, takeoff, climb
         and a 45-minute reserve at 45% power.)
Gross weight . . . . 3850 pounds
Empty weight (includes standard avionics) . . . . 2338 pounds
Useful load . . . . 1528 pounds

Stall speed (landing, full flaps) . . . . 66 MPH
Rate of climb at sea level . . . . 1049 feet per minute
Service ceiling . . . . above 25,000 feet

Maximum altitude limitation . . . . 25,000 feet
Airspeed limits   Maneuvering . . . . 162 MPH
                 Maximum structural cruising . . . . 193 MPH
                 Never exceed . . . . 237 MPH
                 Flaps extended (normal) . . . . 144 MPH
                 Landing gear extended (normal) . . . . 177 MPH
Fuel . . . . 100/130 octane minimum

240

The 1989 B36-TC Bonanza had the same interior and exterior paint design as the 1988 model. Serial numbers were EA-489 through EA-500 . . . a total of 12 units. The Power Plant was the Continental TSIO-520-UB rated at 300 H.P. The standard equipped price in 1989 was $264,800.

THESE CHANGES OCCURRED DURING PRODUCTION:

- Cowl assembly skin thickness change, E-494 and after,
- Fuel strainer placard change, E-493 and after.

B36-TC

BONANZA

MODEL YEAR 1990

Performance with the turbocharged TSIO-520-UB:

Top speed at 19,000 feet . . . . 245 MPH
Maximum recommended cruise power . . . . 79% (237 HP)
Cruise speed at 79% power at 25,000 feet
    full throttle, 2500 RPM. . . . . 230 MPH
Standard fuel capacity . . . . 108 gallons total, usable is 102 gallons
Maximum range (at 196 MPH at 25,000 feet)
    with standard tanks . . . . 1133 miles
(Range includes allowance for warm-up, taxi, takeoff, climb
      and a 45-minute reserve at 45% power.)
Gross weight . . . . 3850 pounds
Empty weight (includes standard avionics) . . . . 2338 pounds
Useful load . . . . 1528 pounds

Stall speed (landing, full flaps) . . . . .66 MPH
Rate of climb at sea level . . . . 1049 feet per minute
Service ceiling . . . . above 25,000 feet

Maximum altitude limitation . . . . 25,000 feet
Airspeed limits   Maneuvering . . . . 162 MPH
                  Maximum structural cruising. . . . . 193 MPH
                  Never exceed. . . . . 237 MPH
                  Flaps extended (normal) . . . . 144 MPH
                  Landing gear extended (normal) . . . . 177 MPH
Fuel . . . . 100/130 octane minimum

The 1990 B36-TC Bonanza had the same interior and exterior paint design as the 1989 model. Serial numbers began with EA-501 and ended with EA-513 . . . a total of 13 units. The Power Plant is the Continental TSIO-520-UB rated at 300 H.P. The standard equipped price is $288,500.

THIS CHANGE OCCURRED DURING PRODUCTION:

- Air conditioner time delay change, EA-512 and after.

Photo courtesy of Edward H. Phillips.

MODEL T36-TC
(EXPERIMENTAL)

I talked to five different Beechcrafters and got five different answers as to why this airplane was not put into production. At the time Beech was considering both a pressurized and an unpressurized version. I was told by one source that there were some minor, short-term control problems similar to those Piper experienced with the T-Tail Lance. These surely could have been overcome. The airplane's C.G. range must have been a beaut with that 12″ extension forward of the windshield.

I came away from these conversations with the feeling that there was not a strong marketing push behind it. The development program on the Lightning may have contributed to its demise. It's a shame, because those of us in the field liked it.

Beech engineers modified a basic Model A36 Bonanza fuselage with a newly designed T-Tail for experimental flight testing intended to investigate the feasibility of a pressurized, single-engine Bonanza. Designated c/n EC-1 (N2065T) the T36-TC was an unpressurized test-bed powered by a 325 hp Continental TSIO-520 engine with aft-mounted turbocharger, requiring a 12-inch extension forward of the windshield to accommodate the power-plant. The T36-TC made its first flight February 16, 1979 with Beech engineering test pilots Lou Johansen and Robert Suter at the controls. A total of 82 hours, 45 minutes of testing were accumulated during 89 flights, with the last flight made on January 25, 1980. T36-TC illustrated flown by Lou Johansen.

Beechcraft Lightning, a turbine-powered pressurized single-engine aircraft.

Preliminary Performance Estimates	
Model Designation	38P
Engine	P & W PT6A-40
Gross Weight (lbs)	5800
Max. Certificated Altitude (ft)	25,000
Maximum Cruise Power @ 25,000 ft. True Airspeed - Knots (mph)	282 (325)
Range* - Nautical (statute)	934 (1075)
Maximum Range Power @ 25,000 ft. True Airspeed - Knots (mph)	210 (242)
Range* - Nautical (statute)	1182 (1360)
*Flyover range w/45 minute reserve	

This airplane was to be manufactured with three engines:
A Pratt & Whitney PT6A-130, that would cruise at 230 knots (265 mph) plus.
A Pratt & Whitney PT6A-40, that would cruise at 275 knots (317 mph) plus.
A Garrett AiResearch TPE-331 that would cruise at 235 knots (270 mph) plus.

I think I know what happened with this project even though I had been gone from the factory for some time. This product started out under Hedrick. In my opinion, Engineering, Procurement, Accounting, Cost Control, all told Frank what they thought he wanted to hear. Along comes the new President, Linden Blue. A good looking, likeable guy — they are dying to tell him what they think he wants to hear. That's how the price went from $495,000 to $935,000. The orders on hand disappeared, one of them was ours.

Beechcraft Lightning 38P.

VOYAGER BONANZA

New Liquid-cooled Conversion Program for Bonanzas
Teledyne Continental Motors offers upgrade.

Over the last several months, news of the Teledyne Continental Motors (TCM) liquid-cooled conversion program for the Bonanza has been of great interest to many ABS members. The conversion was seen by several ABS members who attended a Service Clinic in Mobile, Ala. this spring.

The Beechcraft Bonanza conversion program consists of the addition of a Voyager T-550 liquid-cooled engine, a new propeller and redesigned engine cowl. The Voyager T-550 is a turbocharged engine capable of producing 300 hp at its maximum 2500 rpm.

The Voyager conversion program is being offered as an upgrade. Reduced climb fuel consumption, higher altitude capability, reduced pilot workload, reduced cabin noise and longer engine life are all benefits provided by the Voyager conversion

The Voyager engines employ a TCM patented liquid-cooled cylinder design which provides lower operating temperatures and more uniform engine cooling. These advancements in design greatly enhance the longevity of the engine, giving it a 2000 hour TBO.

Other advantages of the liquid-cooling design developed by TCM are better fuel efficiency, higher altitude capability and better wear characteristics. Increased fuel efficiency is achieved, in part, through reduced cooling drag which is the result of aerodynamically refined air inlets on the engine cowls.

The Voyager conversion is now being made available as a retrofit for the A36 Bonanza. Following FAA approval—expected around mid-year

1990—TCM hopes to broaden the scope of the modification to include the Beech Models F33A, V35 and B36TC.

For the time being, conversions are only being made at the factory in Mobile at a price of $78,000. Sometime in the future it is anticipated that TCM will license outside facilities to do the work. *TCM is accepting refundable $5,000 deposits for guaranteed delivery positions.*

In summary, those who choose to make an investment in the new liquid-cooled engine retrofit will get a turbocharged 300 hp engine with a 2000-hour TBO (some company officials believe it could be 3000 hours), a new three-bladed prop, an aerodynamically redesigned engine cowl, plus some special equipment forward of the fire-wall, including cooling pump, plumbing and heat exchanger.

The results of the Voyager Conversion are examined on specification and performance tables included with this article.

Teledyne Continental Motors is one

Beechcraft Bonanza powered by Teledyne Continental Motors' Voyager T-550 liquid-cooled engine.

Teledyne Continental Motors Voyager T-550, 6-cylinder 300-horsepower engine designed specifically for the Beech Bonanza liquid-cooled engine conversion program.

of the world's foremost producers of piston engines for general aviation aircraft. The company's headquarters is located on the Brookley Industrial Complex in Mobile, Ala.

The company has played a key role in developing and manufacturing aircraft engines, pioneering such innovations as dual ignition, fuel injection, turbocharging, hydraulic tappets and reduction gearing.

Over the past 60 years, TCM has improved manufacturing methods by introducing new machining techniques, exacting quality control standards, and hundreds of other upgraded processes. As a result, the reliability and maintainability of TCM's expanding line of engines has been steadily enhanced.

TCM maintains a worldwide distribution network for its new and factory rebuilt engines and has established a warehouse and distribution outlet in Atlanta, Ga., which maintains an inventory of 2,500,000 aircraft engine parts and components.

Voyager® T-550 Engine

Rated Horsepower 300
Rated rpm 2500
Max Cruise Power 250
Max Cruise rpm 2500
Number of cylinders 6
Displacement (cu. in.) ...... 550 in.
Prop Drive .... Direct
Compression Ratio 7.5:1
Bore (inches) 5.25
Stroke (inches) 4.25
Dry Weight (pounds 450
Fuel .... 100 or 100LL
Recommended Oil ..... Mobil AV-1
Coolant .... 60% Ethylene Glycol
TBO .... 2000 hours

Aircraft Performance (Estimated)

Cruise Speed
Max Cruise (250 hp) .... 200 kts
Fuel Burn .... 16.5 gph

75% .... 195 kts
Fuel Burn .... 15.5 gph

65% .... 188 kts
Fuel Burn .... 14.0 gph

Range*
75% .... 715 nm
65% .... 746 nm
55% .... 800 nm

Takeoff ** .... 2,000 ft
Rate of Climb** .... 1100 fpm

*Range includes Start, Taxi, Cruise Climb and 45-minute Reserve
** Over 50 ft. Obstacle @ Gross Weight, Sea Level

General Motors Announces — news about PropJet flying

We at Allison Gas Turbine Division are excited about our new venture - converting A36 Bonanzas to turbine power. We know there are many pilots, Bonanza-based or otherwise, who are excited about the prospect of "slipping the surly bonds of earth" a little bit faster. To this elite group, and to all the pilots who, for commerce or pleasure, deal regularly with short fields or high altitudes, we dedicate this newsletter. We will regularly inform you about a new transportation bonanza - the Prop-Jet Bonanza. There will be news about how it flies, who's flying it, and the records it sets. PropJet Bonanza will give you insights into this new world of "star class" transportation.

PropJet BONANZA

A36 turbine debut heralds new business flying era

The 'new era' of single prop-jet flying has been sneaking up on us. Single prop-jets have been in use by the military for many years and under development in Europe since the mid 1960s. In the U.S. commercial market, the new Cessna Caravan is a single prop-jet heavy hauler; the Soloy conversion of the Cessna 206 is a bush pilot's dream. But when does the 'new era' start for the businessman pilot?

It starts now! It starts with the Prop-Jet Bonanza conversion kit for the A36 straight-tailed six-place Bonanza. It starts as soon as the business flyer with a Bonanza gives up his wings for a five-week conversion to smooth, reliable, economical turbine power.

It starts in mid-December, 1985, when Allison Gas Turbine Division of General Motors is targeted to receive FAA certification of the Prop-Jet conversion.

If "new era" seems strong, consider these new dimensions of single engine business flying.

1. The Prop-Jet Bonanza takes off in just over half the distance required by the piston version. This means extra confidence in take offs from short fields, and at high altitudes.
2. It lands in less than half the distance used by its piston cousin. This desirable feature opens up many small fields to the prop-jet pilot, making out-of-the-way customer calls and intimate vacation spots more convenient. (see page 4)
3. The Prop-Jet climbs at twice the rate of the piston driven bonanza. You get to cruising altitude faster.
4. Annoying engine vibration is a thing of the past. Crew and passengers ride in a new dimension of comfort.

Left: Looking sleek with its new long cowling and winglets, one of the Prop-Jet Bonanza demonstration models cruises effortlessly toward another speed record.

Transition to prop-jet flying—simply exciting

The excitement starts when Jack Schweibold taxies up to the ramp where you're waiting for your demo ride. Years of listening to burbling exhaust sounds do not prepare you for the melodious hum of the idling turbine.

You like Bonanzas, but this one has new appeal. The addition of the long nose is subtle, but adds a certain sleekness to the craft. The tip tanks and rakish winglets give it almost a military jet look.

The first step in your transition is the pre-flight inspection. Nothing much different. An extra tip tank on each side to drain check. Everything external aft of the firewall remains effectively the same. Landing gear, flaps, and control surfaces are all unchanged.

You check oil level and make sure there are no birds nesting in the air intake under the spinner. The reversible three-bladed Hartzell prop is a bit different, but adds a rugged look.

You're ready to step inside. Vintage Bonanza again, with only a change in engine gauges and controls. Gone is the mixture control; two levers replace the three you're used to.

Starting the turbine is simplicity itself. There is little difference between starting procedure whether the climate is hot or cold. You monitor only two gauges throughout the start procedure. N1 (compressor speed) and TOT (Turbine outlet temperature) give you all the informaion you need.

Turbine Outlet Temperature, limiting factor in turbine operation, is indicated on the TOT gage (top). Compressor speed is read in per cent of maximum on the lower gage.

Push the "Start" button down. It is spring loaded so it stays in position. When compressor speed reaches 15%, advance the condition lever. Monitor TOT and keep it below 927° C. When N1 shows 60% and positive oil pressure is indicated, return the start switch to OFF position. The engine is now at idle.

You're up and running. Next, activate the generator, avionics, and electrical switches. Following the start, the Prop-Jet Bonanza becomes a one lever aircraft. The condition lever (prop speed) remains at 100% throughout the flight; the power lever is used to make all power changes.

On the prototype PropJet, the old T,P,M markings (for throttle, pitch, and mixture) show the positioning of the new Condition Lever (right) and Power Lever (left).

Ground control releases you to taxi to the active and you advance the pitch control to take a bite of air. The turbine purrs along at idle. As you roll out a bit fast, Jack suggests trying the Beta Range (reverse prop pitch) technique for slowing down. Some pilots like to use it to preserve their brakes. It does have the advantage that the prop is working for you through all taxi phases.

Run up is accomplished by advancing the power lever to 85% prop speed and depressing the overspeed test button. The propeller speed will decrease similar to cycling the prop on a piston aircraft. With the propeller over speed test complete and all gauges in green, you're ready for flight.

Tower says "Position and Hold", then "Five Zero Alpha Tango cleared for takeoff, hold runway heading to 2000 feet, contact Departure Control on 126.0." You advance the power level until "take off" power is attained, indicated by a reading of 810 on the TOT. You are shoved back in your seat by the acceleration.

Jack's instructions were, "Rotate at 65 knots and hold about 20 degrees pitch to climb out at 90." That's hard to do because you're not accustomed to a 20 degree climb angle. You try it anyway and experience a 2000 foot per minute climb. You're at 800 feet before you have the gear up and at 1500 feet crossing the end of the 8500 foot runway.

Takeoff power is maintained for five minutes, then the condition lever is pulled back to give a TOT reading of 757 degrees. This is normal climb power.

Climbing to 12,000 feet in less than six minutes is new experience for the single engine business pilot, but one you're bound to enjoy. To set cruise power, pull back on the power lever until TOT reads 738 degrees.

Putting Prop-Jet Bonanza through its paces reveals the smoothest and quietest single you've ever flown. To start a descent, reduce power to hold 166 KIAS, then adjust power to achieve the desired rate of descent. A typical descent requires about a 30% power reduction to 40-50 psi torque. You'll learn to think "torque" instead of "manifold pressure".

We do a normal descent, although the turbine is tolerant of rapid descent (no worry about cooling too fast) and the approach is routine. Routine, until we touch the wheels. Then, a quick pull back on the power lever and we are snubbed to a stop by the reversed prop after a landing roll of less than 400 feet.

Now, advance the power lever back to ground idle. Play with the Beta Range braking on the way in and give the bystanders a show by backing up to park.

Shut down is simple. After turning of the avionics, electrical circuits, and generator, simply pull the position lever all the way back. This action shuts off fuel and stops the combustion of jet fuel. N1 and prop spool down to a stop. A truly remarkable first flight is over. The piston pilot will have a glow of accomplishment, a feeling of discovery, and a severe case of "more!"

World Speed Records — Proof of Concept

Proof of concept can take many forms. Setting new world class speed records is one way the Allison Gas Turbine team is proving the capabilities of the A36 Bonanza powered by the Allison 250-B17 turbine.

As Bonanza 7214D is ferried around the country for demos and air shows, some routine flights generate world speed records. That's the nature of Prop Jet Bonanza: Trend Setter; Record Setter.

From July 25 to September 19, five FAI world speed records were recorded

7/25/85   Indianapolis to Oshkosh   230.86 mph

Jay Penner flew with Mark Schweibold as co-pilot to exhibit 7214D at the EAA Convention and Fly in.

8/21/85 Indianapolis to Washington DC 240.96 mph

Jack Schweibold and Larry Chambers co-captained the flight with Fritz Harvey as co-pilot. They cruised at 18,000 feet, making the trip in just over two hours.

9/14/85   Reno (Closed course)   237.00 mph

Larry Chambers and Marie McMillan co-captained this demonstration run around the fifteen mile closed course during the 1985 Reno Air Races.

9/15/85   Reno to Indianapolis   221.24 mph

Jack Schweibold and Larry Chambers were co-captains on the trip "home" from Reno. The record setting trip included a stop at Goodland, Kansas.

9/19/85   Wichita to Indianapolis   236.00 mph

Returning from a visit to Beech Aircraft, Mick Molish joined Jack Schweibold in recording a 236.00 mph mark.

Jack Schweibold, Manager of the A36 Conversion project for Allison Gas Turbine Division, points to new world speed records being added to the record map at Allison Flight Operations, Indianapolis. A number of the records belong to turbine powered helicopters, but the PropJet Bonanza is quickly filling the map with fixed wing records.

Larry Chambers and Marie McMillan are interviewed for Reno television after setting the new 15/25 Km closed course speed record during the 1985 Reno Air Races.

Larry Chambers, Marie McMillan, and Jack Schweibold get star treatment from the Reno Air Race crowd as they parade with a race official after receiving recognition for their new closed course speed record. McMillan, who co-piloted the speed run with Chambers, has the distinction of holding more individual speed records than any other pilot.

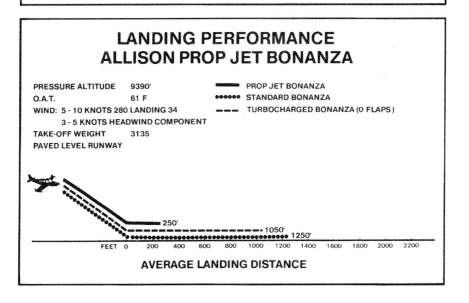

TAKE-OFF PERFORMANCE
ALLISON PROP JET BONANZA

PRESSURE ALTITUDE   9390'

O.A.T.   61 F

WIND: 5 - 10 KNOTS 280 LANDING 34

     3 - 5 KNOTS HEADWIND COMPONENT

TAKE-OFF WEIGHT   3135

PAVED LEVEL RUNWAY

▬▬▬ PROP JET BONANZA

●●●●●● STANDARD BONANZA

▬ ▬ ▬ ■ TURBOCHARGED BONANZA (0 FLAPS)

1100'

1800'

2100'

0 FEET   200   400   600   800   1000   1200   1400   1600   1800   2000   2200   2400

AVERAGE TAKE-OFF DISTANCE

LANDING PERFORMANCE
ALLISON PROP JET BONANZA

PRESSURE ALTITUDE   9390'

O.A.T.   61 F

WIND: 5 - 10 KNOTS 280 LANDING 34

     3 - 5 KNOTS HEADWIND COMPONENT

TAKE-OFF WEIGHT   3135

PAVED LEVEL RUNWAY

▬▬▬ PROP JET BONANZA

●●●●●● STANDARD BONANZA

▬ ▬ ▬ TURBOCHARGED BONANZA (0 FLAPS)

250'

1050'

1250'

FEET   0   200   400   600   800   1000   1200   1400   1600   1800   2000   2200

AVERAGE LANDING DISTANCE

251

Showing off the PropJet Bonanza

Pictures and spec sheets are fine, but there is no substitute for seeing the Prop-Jet Bonanza "in the flesh". Since mid-1984, over one thousand pilots have taken demonstration flights in two prototype Prop-Jet Bonanzas.

N250AT is the first conversion. A 1979 Bonanza, its conversion and flight testing helped set the parameters for the final conversion kit configuration. Aircraft #2 is N7214D. It was purchased off the demonstrator line and converted

to prop-jet power using a kit developed from the early test flight experience.

The Prop-Jet Bonanza has been seen at Oshkosh, Flying Physicians convention in Sun Valley, American Bonanza Society conventions, and many statewide meets.

Allison's Prop-Jet Bonanza was exhibited at the Reno Air Races, at the NBAA Convention in New Orleans, and at the AOPA Convention in Washington DC.

If you missed the chance to preview the Prop-Jet Bonanza at a major show, drop a note to Larry Chambers and he'll keep you informed when one of the two prototypes will be in your area.

Write to:

Larry Chambers, A36 Sales Manager
Allison Gas Turbine Division
4101 B Dandy Trail
Indianapolis, IN 46254

Rave notices at Oshkosh
At an event where "oohs" and "aahs" abount, the PropJet Bonanza got high marks for drama from the visitors at the Experimental Aviation Association Fly-in at Oshkosh in July, 1985. Knowledgeable pilots recognized the A36, then did a double-take at the long nose and winglets. The real "oohs" and "aahs" started when they scanned the performance charts.

One of the most severe requirements for the A36 Turbine Conversion was the atmospheric icing test series. To find suitable conditions, the PropJet Bonanza was flown to Yellowknife, Northwest Territories, Canada, for eight days of testing for intake ice accumulation and turbine operation under icing conditions.

STC — the Supplemental Type Certificate

Although it flies like a new aircraft, the Prop-Jet Bonanza will be converted under a Supplemental Type Certificate, a thorough FAA certification that takes into account the aircraft's original airframe certification. This procedure, while cutting years from the certification of a completely new aircraft, carries the same authority to build as the original Manufacturer's Type Certificate.

Because the Prop-Jet Bonanza requires a new cowling, new engine mounts, tip tanks, and winglets, some fuselage stress testing was required. The result: all design parameters were achieved with excellent margins.

Besides extensive static and systems tests, over a thousand flight test hours have been flown on the installation.

Performance - the Bottom Line

Replacing the piston engine with the Allison 250 turbine does much more than add to the cruising speed. The benefits of turbine power go far beyond speed, adding safety, useful load, high altitude capability, and short field performance.

Useful Load:	**1440 pounds (up from 1149)**
Take-off roll:	**550 ft. (sea level/standard)**
Landing roll:	**350 Ft. (sea level/standard)**
Service ceiling:	**25,000 ft.**
Range:	**1100nm**

Tip tank - tip off that you're flying the Prop-Jet Bonanza
*Except when directly abeam, people you pass in the air would have little in-
dication that you are flying the new Star Class PropJet Bonanza were it not
for its jaunty tip tanks and winglets. They are not just there for the looks. The
winglet and tiptanks provide stability, working as gates to increase air flow
over ailerons. They also give the Allison team a billboard for showing off the
total hours flown. This photo, over Grand Canyon, was made en route to Reno
Air Races.*

Dealer network underway

Where can I place my order? Where do I pick up my PropJet conversion?? Allison Gas Turbine Division of General Motors is the initial marketing agency for the conversion, but dealerships are now being assigned.

Because every FBO may not have valid prospects for the Prop Jet speedster, dealerships are currently being limited to those agencies with both interest AND immediate prospects. Dealers may sign their first order (a requisite for dealer status) for their own use, for demonstration purposes, or for customer delivery.

Until orders exceed capacity, conversions will be made by Soloy Conversions, Olympia, Washington. An owner may take delivery at Olympia (great vacation country) or have his PropJet Bonanza ferried to his home port. For dealership particulars, call Jack Schweibold, A36 Project Manager at (317) 242-3120.

PropJet BONANZA

Prop-Jet Bonanza is published by the Allison Gas Turbine Division of General Motors Corporation for the sole purpose of informing pilots and aviation enthusiasts about the progress of the A36 Turbine Conversion Project.

PropJet BONANZA

Allison Gas Turbine Division
General Motors Corporation
4101B Dandy Trail
Indianapolis In 46254

Larrie Chambers flying Allison Turbine conversion. I sold this A36 to Allison. It was the last Bonanza I sold while at Indiana Beechcraft. This picture was taken near Scottsdale, Arizona, January 1, 1986. Larrie Chambers worked for me three times, twice as Service Manager, the last time as a Salesman.

From Beechcraft Preliminary Design, Bonanza and Travel Air Concepts, 1946 through 1968

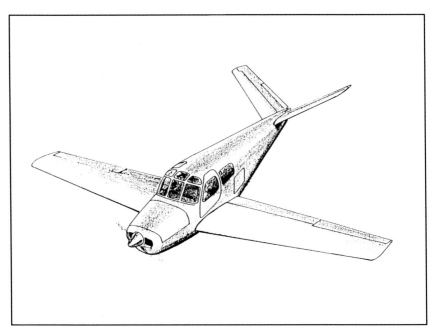

PD38 Wide Body Bonanza — July, 1946.

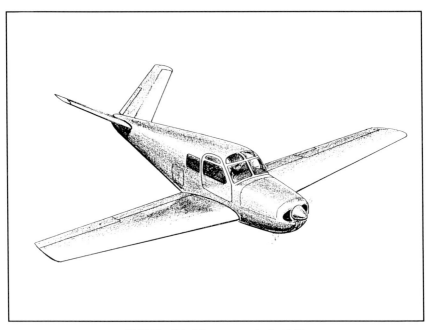

PD39 Flat Sided Bonanza — April, 1947.

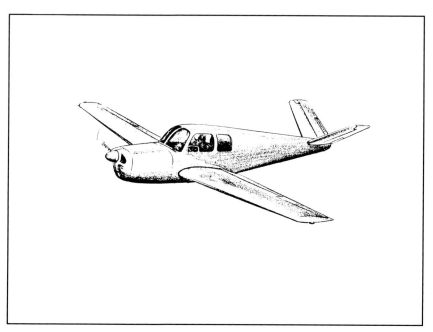

PD40 Bonanza With Twin Engines/One Propeller — 1947.

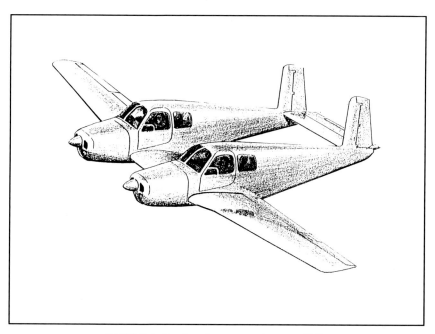

PD49A Twin Fuselage Bonanza — January, 1948.

PD49 Twin Engine Bonanza — April, 1949.

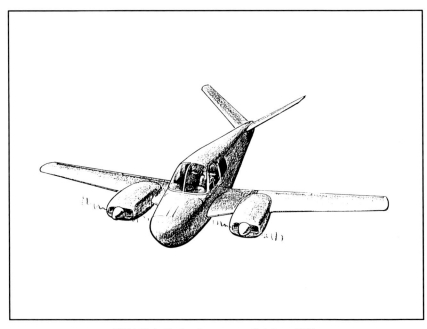

PD61 Twin Engine Bonanza — October, 1953.

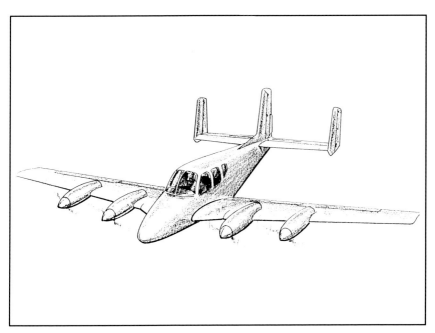

PD117-1 4-Engine Travelair (Turboprop) — May, 1957.

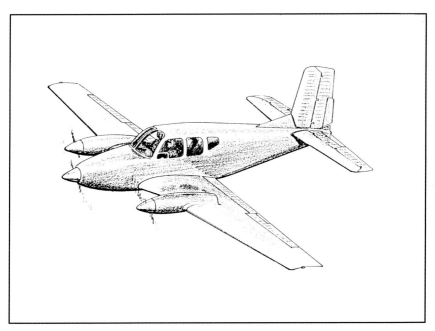

PD117-3 Travelair 3-Engine (Turboprop) — May, 1957.

PD150-1 "Modular" Cabin - 33 Tail — October, 1959.

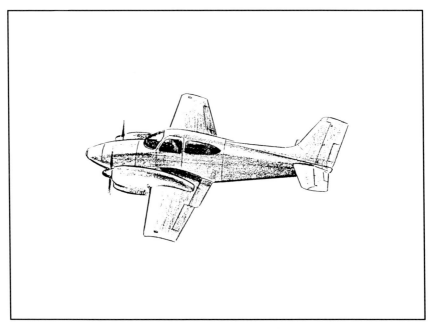

PD153 Model 95 With Modular Cabin — October, 1959.

PD156 30° Sweep on L.E. Of Bonanza "V" Tail — November, 1959.

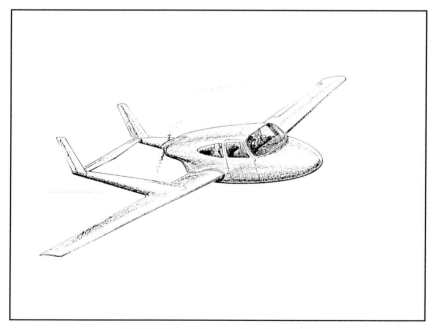

PD155 4-Place Pusher — November, 1959.

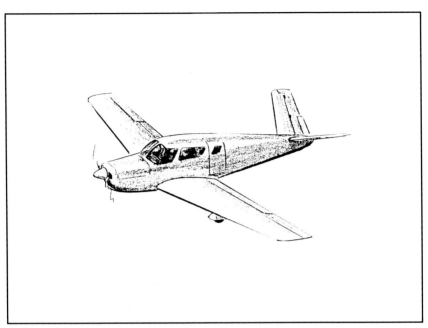

PD152-2 Model 35 With Modular (Common) Cabin — November, 1959.

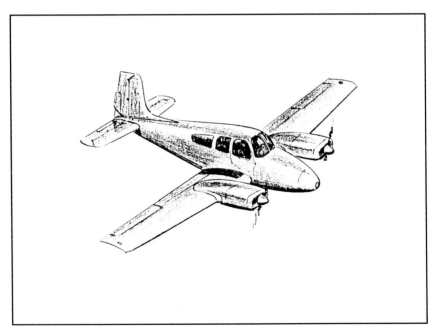

PD154-1 Model C95A With New Wing — January, 1960.

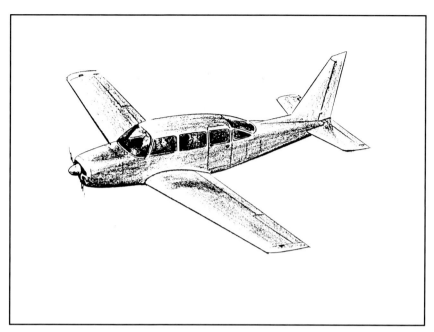

PD167 Bonanza Fuselage — July, 1960.

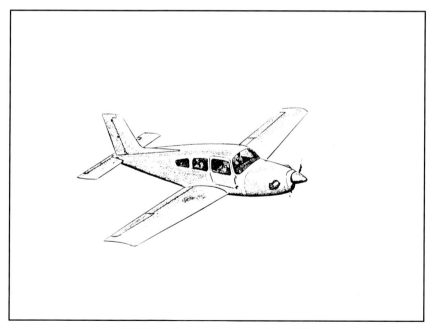

PD189-1-1 Bonanza Replacement — 1963.

PD206 (PD207, Modified PD206) Turbocharged/Pressurized Single Engine — January, 1965.

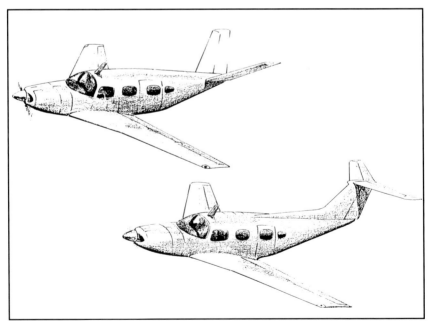

PD221 4-6 Place Bonanza Replacement — 1967.

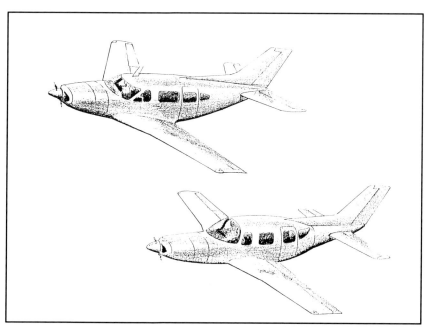

PD221 6-Place Bonanza Replacement — 1967.

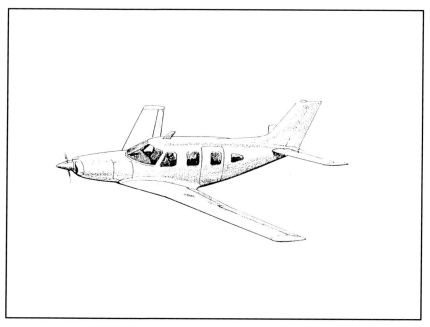

PD221 Bonanza Replacement (Pressurized) — 1967.

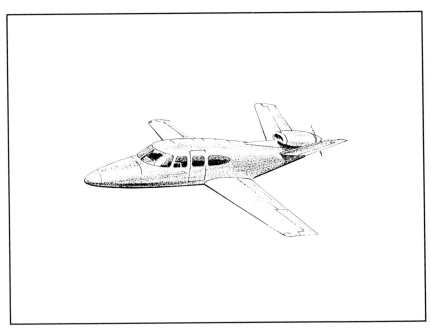

PD221 6-Place Bonanza Replacement — 1967.

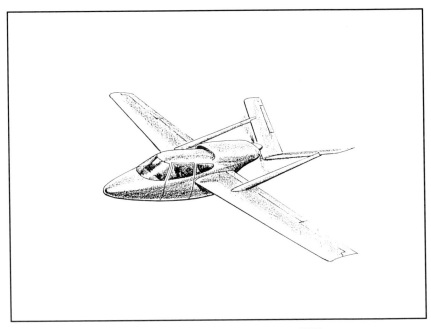

PD221 6-Place Bonanza Replacement — 1967.

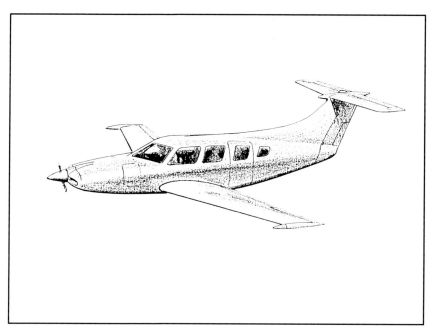

PD221 6-Place Bonanza Replacement (Styled) — November, 1968.

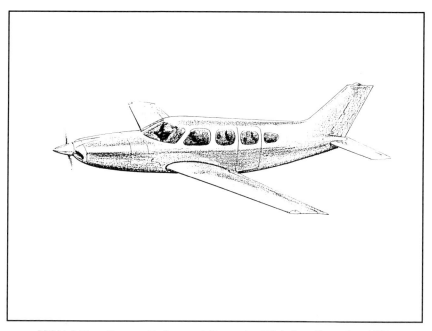

PD221 6-Place Bonanza Replacement (Pressurized/Styled) — November, 1968.

The Art Department's Jet Bonanza.

We Get Letters . . .

The following are letters I received after my first book *Those Incomparable Bonanzas,* was published. I think of particular interest is the letter from "Roosh Naidenoff, who at the time worked for the AiResearch Manufacturing Company of Arizona, a Division of the Garrett Corporation. You might have been flying a Culver Bonanza!

Here are the words of the people who were there.

AIRESEARCH MANUFACTURING COMPANY OF ARIZONA

A DIVISION OF THE GARRETT CORPORATION

SKY HARBOR AIRPORT • 402 SOUTH 36TH STREET • PHOENIX, ARIZONA 85034

TELEPHONE 267-3011

22 January 1971

Mr. Larry A. Ball
9407 Peach Tree Lane
Wichita, Kansas 67207

Dear Larry:

I have read your manuscript and find it pretty accurate. There are a few points of interest I would like to bring out that you may want to insert between some of the statements that you have already made.

We did start with a two-place airplane and ended with a four-place, but the amazing part of it was that the airplane's size did not grow very much. We kept squeezing people and equipment in without enlarging the size of the fuselage. After we designed the cabin for four people to sit comfortably, we ran out of space for equipment. For instance, we needed a fuel selector valve and a wobble pump within the pilot's reach. There was space available for one, but not the other; so we designed our own selector valve and pump into one unit which was considerably smaller and lighter than either one of the available commercial units.

Another problem that occurred was with the oil tank and oil cooler. We had room for one, but not the other. The oil tank was designed first and the cooler was added inside the oil tank. The cooler was designed to function by gravity feed only and not pressure. Therefore, a lightweight assembly was possible. The combination oil tank and cooler weighed 4½ lbs. total, but if a commercial cooler was used with the required external plumbing, the weight of the system would have been in excess of 30 lbs.

While I was having trouble finding the proper lightweight equipment for the power plant, Ralph Harmon was having the same problem with the instrument panel. There were no lightweight instruments available and certainly none that had any style. Ralph worked hard on various instrument manufacturers and even designed some of his own and, in the end, he did design a lightweight instrument panel that was quite stylish.

To have four people fit comfortably in such a small airplane, some established laws of aerodynamics have to be broken. The one that bothered us the most was the C.G. travel of the Bonanza. It had far greater C.G. travel than was acceptable in aircraft at that time, but thanks to Jerry Gordon's wind tunnel tests,

SYSTEMS AND COMPONENTS FOR: AIRCRAFT, MISSILE, SPACECRAFT, ELECTRONIC, NUCLEAR AND INDUSTRIAL APPLICATIONS

270

additions were made to the wings and tail which eliminated any bad flight characteristics of the Bonanza whether it was flown empty or full.

You asked what did Walter Beech think of the Bonanza. When it was time to present the Bonanza program to the Board of Directors, Beech Aircraft was already involved in some major programs such as the Twin Quad airplane, the C18S airplane, a new stagger wing airplane, an electric car, an all aluminum house (which was called Dymaxium) and some other minor programs.

Ralph Harmon was called to the Board Room to make the pitch on the Bonanza. After a couple of hours, the Board decided that the Bonanza was too small an airplane for Beech Aircraft. They were going to do bigger and better things. Mr. Beech did not say much during the presentation or during the discussions, but when he saw which way the decision was going, he turned to Ralph Harmon and said "If these people don't want to build it here, bring it to Culver Aviation Company and we will build it there." Mr. Beech had some personal money invested in Culver at that time. When the Board Members realized the way Mr. Beech felt, they reluctantly decided to change their minds and gave an O.K. for the Bonanza program.

I obtained the above story secondhanded. To get exactly what happened in the Board Room, I wish you would call Ralph Harmon at Aerostar, Inc. at Kerrville, Texas. I am sure he would gladly fill in the details.

Another point of interest, of all the programs that I mentioned above, the only one that was successful was the Beech Bonanza.

Larry, I hope I have given you a little something to add to your manuscript. If you need clarification on anything, please let me know.

Sincerely,

Roosh Naidenoff

RN:ms

Pat Boling.

UNITED AIR LINES

San Francisco International Airport, San Francisco, California 94128

MAINTENANCE BASE

2-25-72

Dear Mr. Bell -

I've just been browsing through a friend's copy of your book. Will you mail me a copy? I could not find a price on it, so please bill me.

I would be flattered if you would autograph it, too.

Pat Boling

(Manila - Pendleton via Beech Bonanza)

Flight Operations

United Air Lines, Int'l Airport SFO 94128

16301 Plummer Street
Sepulveda, California 91343

January 17, 1972

Mr. Larry Ball
8407 Peach Tree Lane
Wichita, Kansas 67207

Dear Larry:

I read and enjoyed your article in the January "Private Pilot".
It was very good. I would like to get an autographed copy of
your book "Those Incomparable Bonanzas". I am enclosing a copy
of an article I have written. If any of the material in my
article is of any help to you, please feel free to use it.

Have you seen a booklet entitled "Bonanza Facts" by Dr. B. J.
McClanahan and published by Empire City Directories, P. O. Box 13,
Hornell, N. Y? On page 4 it mentions my incident.

Good luck with your book.

Sincerely,

Bob

Robert R. King

Walter Beech with Harry Reiter — 1946.

Preproduction experimental Bonanza Crash. Harry Reiter and Robert King.

MR. ~~& MRS~~. ROBERT R. KING
16301 Plummer Street
Sepulveda, Calif. 913~~10~~ 43
9-7-71

THE DAY I MET MY PERSONAL SAVIOR

The first streaks of dawn were just beginning to show as we taxied out
for our take-off from the Beech Aircraft Airport. This was a critical test
and the only remaining test to be completed before the Beech Bonanza could
be licensed by the Civil Aeronautics Authority (now FAA). The test was a
terminal velocity dive, which meant that we started at altitude, pointed the
nose toward the ground and dove until we reached "redline" (maximum) airspeed.
Then, if no trouble developed, we would level out, slow up and return to the
factory for examination of the airplane and data evaluation. This was
October 26, 1946. The Bonanza was a newly designed light, four passenger
plane with revolutionary features, such as the V-tail. There had been problems
during development but now, hopefully, there would be no more problems during
the terminal velocity dive and the airplane would be certified.

We had, in fact, had previous problems with the terminal velocity dive.
Just the afternoon before the Pilot, Harry Reiter and I (the Flight Engineer
and Pilot) had made a terminal velocity dive. As we had approached "redline",
we felt as though a large airbrake slowed us down. We pulled out of the dive
and landed. We found that the right landing gear door had somehow come partly
open during the dive and the airstream had bent it back so it did, indeed,
act as a large air brake to slow the airplane down. We had hurriedly called
Ralph Harmon, Project Engineer for the Bonanza, and Jerry Gordon, Chief Aerodynamist, to look at the damaged landing gear door. It was finally decided
to install a reinforced landing gear door and to rig it so it would close
tighter.

Harry and I had all these things in mind as we ran through the take-off
checklist. It had been a long and busy engineering flight test program on
this new airplane, so we were eager to complete the final test. We were
making this critical test so early in the morning because the air was more
likely to be smooth. The pre-flight complete, we made our take-off to the
south, turned east and made a maximum climb to 12,000 feet. At this altitude,
we leveled off and checked to be sure we were ready for the dive. Harry was
in the left seat and I was in the right seat. There was only one door and
it was beside me. It was a quick release door, i.e, you could pull a lever
and the door would release and fall free, away from the airplane. We were

276

MR. & MRS. ROBERT R. KING
16301 Plummer Street
Sepulveda, Calif. 91350 43
9-7-71

both wearing new 24-foot, back pack parachutes, as this was still an "X"
(Experimental) airplane. Finally, we were satisfied we were ready. I said
to Harry, "You call out the airspeed". Harry said, "O.K., here we go" and
pointed the nose down. "180, 190.. 200, 210, 220...". Harry was calling
out the airspeed and I was busy recording data. All of a sudden there was
a very loud cracking sound and the airplane rolled violently to the right and
upside down! There were more cracking sounds and great confusion as the
airplane started to violently tumble.

The altimeter was in front of me and was unwinding so fast I could not
read it. Things are very confused because of the airplane's wild gyrations,
but I realized we had to get out of the airplane right now. I said to
Harry, "I'm going out... Do you need help?" Harry replied, "I can get out
all right... You go ahead". After that things were so confused, it is
difficult to remember anything too clearly, but I do remember two things
very clearly. I made a short prayer, committing myself to my God. I had an
immediate answer in the form of a feeling of well being... a feeling of relief,
that everything would be all right. The second thing I remember is tumbling
about the cabin as the plane gyrated through the sky. I do not remember
having released my safety belt, though I must have. I do remember lying across
the top of the cabin, with my legs toward the tail and my head and neck jammed
down into the instrument panel. I remember how much my neck hurt and then
I must have 'blacked out' for the next thing I remember is that it was quiet
and peaceful, without all that banging and cracking noise but the earth was
still gyrating around me and I was by myself. I suddenly realized I was falling
through space! The air was rushing by and it felt good because it was cool.
I rejoiced that it was so calm and peaceful yet I knew that I had to hurry to
find the ripcord and open the parachute. Near panic, I could not seem to find
the ripcord though I was searching wildly. Suddenly, the sun glinted off the
chrome ripcord handle! I grabbed it and pulled. To my relief, the chute blossomed
over my head and I was suddenly pulled upright. The shock felt good. The
earth was in its proper place now and I was floating down about 1500 feet from
that frozen Kansas wheat field, and I still had that serene feeling that everything
would be all right.

-2-

277

I had a moment to reflect as to why I could not find the ripcord.
I suddenly realized I had been trying to get the ripcord with my left hand,
since I am naturally left handed, when I should have been using my right hand.
If the sun hadn't shown me that ripcord... still I had the feeling of supreme
confidence that I had never felt so strongly before.

The ground was coming up rapidly now and I could see how fast I was
falling. The north wind was blowing 60 mph and the long thorn hedges were
at least 20 feet high. I was being blown toward a thorn hedge and it looked
as though I would be blown into it. At the last moment I just cleared the top
of the hedge and hit the frozen plowed ground very hard, just downwind of the
hedge. I felt a very sharp pain in my back as I hit the ground hard. Fortunately,
the high, thick hedge cut off the wind so the chute fell to the ground and did
not drag me. I lay on my back, in pain, but thinking how beautiful it was to
be alive and thanking God for his help. I lay there for a while and then I
suddenly realized I was getting cold, as I just had on a cotton flying suit
and cotton jacket. I decided to see if I could get up. It seemed that every
muscle and bone in my body protested, but I finally got on my feet. My back
really hurt. I got out of the parachute harness and was trying to gather up
the chute when two farmers drove into the field. They both jumped out of
their 1935 Ford and came running over to me. They asked me if I was all right
and I said "I guess so". They helped me gather up the chute.

I got in the back seat of their 1935 Ford. I layed down, because I didn't
feel very well, and covered up with the parachute because I was getting a chill.
The farmers took me to a farmhouse, where I tried to call the Beech factory
but nobody answered as it was still too early in the morning. The farmers said
they would take me to Wichita (about 60 miles). I layed down in the back seat
and covered up with the chute again as I was feeling worse all the time. On
the way to Wichita, the farmers told me they had seen the airplane diving, then
come apart in the air, saw me come out and my parachute open. I asked them if
they had seen anything of Harry, but they didn't answer. I thought that was
rather strange but didn't feel like pressing the matter.

When we got to the Beech factory, I thanked the farmers (whose names I still
don't know) and with the parachute bunched in my arms, weht in the main entrance.

-3-

278

As it was still early, the only person in the Main Office was the General Manager, Jack Gaty's secretary. By this time I was very cold, so I asked the secretary if she had any blankets. She said, "No" and asked what happened. I told her briefly and she looked at me as though she couldn't believe my story. I asked her to call the company doctor and also call Nels Fendrich, our other Engineering Test Pilot. I lay down on the couch in Jack Gaty's office. I lay there shivering (from the shock that was setting in) so the secretary came in and put her coat over me.

Nels Fendrich burst into the room (he had run all the way from the experimental hangar) and wanted to know what had happened. The company nurse suddenly appeared and stuck a thermometer in my mouth. I recounted the incident. Nels wanted to know what had happened to Harry and I told him I didn't know. The nurse read the thermometer and hurried back to the first aid room to get some hot water bottles and blankets. I asked Nels to call Faith, my wife, because I was worried that she would hear the news of the accident on the radio and Faith was pregnant with our second child. Nels told Faith briefly about the accident and assured her I was all right. I talked to her and she wanted to come and see me, so I told her it was all right to come.

Jack Gaty came in and I told him all about it, with some help from Nels as I was feeling pretty rotten - chills, stiff and sore. A neighbor brought my wife to the office and I visited with her, assuring her that I was all right. It was decided that I would go to the hospital for X-rays, so I walked out to the company car, carrying the blankets the nurse had given me. Faith went back home and the driver took me to the hospital. I lay on the back seat and covered up with the blankets.

At the hospital they took numerous X-rays and then put me to bed. I was in the hospital the first time from Friday morning (the day of the accident) until Sunday morning. Faith came to see me several times, as often as she could get someone to take care of Carol, our oldest daughter who was then about 18 months old.

Saturday night Nels Fendrich and Elton Rolly (an Engineering Test Pilot for Boeing) came to visit me. I asked Nels what happened to Harry Reiter and he avoided answering me. I didn't feel too well so I didn't press for an answer.

-4-

279

Sunday morning the Beech Company doctor came in. He said the X-rays didn't indicate any problems, so I could go home. I was surprised, as I was so stiff and sore I could not get out of bed without help. I asked the doctor about this and he said it was normal and I would soon get over it. So I called Faith to come and get me. She wasn't feeling well (this accident had been very hard on her) so she called my good friend Jim Close. Jim took me home from the hospital. It was good to be home!

Sunday night about 20 people that worked with me at Beech came over to our house to visit me. I learned from them that Harry had been killed in the accident. They said the farmers had seen his body fall from the plane but his parachute didn't open before he hit the ground. I felt very badly that Harry had been killed and felt sorry for his wife, Ned, and their young son.

On Monday, my parents drove down from Lincoln, Nebraska. Harry's funeral was in the afternoon and my folks baby-sat for us so Faith and I could go. A lot of people that worked with us at Beech were there and it was pretty sad. Harry was quite a guy and the priest said a lot of nice things about him. I was still feeling pretty bad.

Tuesday morning, Jack Gaty called and asked Faith why I wasn't at work. Faith said I didn't feel well enough to go to work. Jack said he was sorry to hear that and he would have the company doctor call me. About 4:00 p.m., Faith was cooking pheasant for dinner, when the company doctor called and said he wanted me taken to the hospital. Faith said she was cooking a special dinner (mostly for my folks) and could I go to the hospital after dinner. The doctor said no, he wanted me at the hospital right away. So my Dad took me to the hospital. I was admitted right away and put to bed. The Beech Compnay doctor came in with an orthopedic surgeon. The surgeon explained that he had looked at my X-rays and there was a crushed disk in my lower back. We learned later that Nancy Johnson, a nurse and wife of Johney Johnson (who worked with me at Beech) had come on duty at the hospital on Monday. She had tried to find me and learned I had been discharged Sunday. She looked up my X-rays and asked the orthopedic surgeon to look at them. He found the crushed disk. Nancy called the nurse at Beech, who had the Beech Company doctor get in touch with the orthopedic surgeon. So I was back in the hospital and this time for a longer stay.

-5-

280

I was in the hospital for six weeks and came home in a body cast from my hips to my neck. Many of the people I worked with came to visit me while I was in the hospital and I was grateful for their concern. I went back to work while I was still in the cast and even did some flying. My most embarrassing moment occured after my cast was removed, when the doctor sent me to a woman's corset shop. All the gals laughed at a man being fitted for a corset!

What did I learn from all this? I am certain that my God pulled me from that plane, helped me open the chute and saved my life. Why was I saved and Harry wasn't? I have not found the answer to that question, but I am firmly convinced that I met my Savior high in the sky and He saved me for some good purpose.

-6-

16301 Plummer Street
Sepulveda Calif. 91343

May 4, 1973

Dr. B. J. McClanahan
St. James Mercy Hospital
411 Canisteo Street
Hornell, N. Y. 14843

Dear Dr. McClanahan:

Thank you for your letter of March 29, 1973. I am happy to answer
your questions to the best of my ability, though I have never written
the numbers down so I have to rely on my memory and it has been since
October 26, 1946 (according to my Caterpillar Club card). You and
Max Karant are right and Larry Ball is wrong. The accident was as I
described it in my story. The airspeed indicator was in front of Harry
Reiter (and he was in the left seat) and the altimeter was in front
of me. I was recording time (since the start of the dive) from a stop
watch, indicated airspeed, indicated altitude and outside air temperature.
Harry was calling out airspeed at every 10 mph and I was writing down
all the readings. As I remember it, we were trying to license the Bonanza
with a redline of 220, with 10% over that if everything felt alright.
I think I had written down 210 (that Harry had called out) and an instant
after that I heard the loud cracking sound that indicated the right wing
failure. So the airspeed at that point must have been between 210 and
220. I was busy watching the instruments and recording, so I didn't
know anything was wrong until I heard that loud crack and felt the violent
roll to the right and then the tumbling.

I ended up in the hospital and finally went back to work in a cast from the
hips to my neck as I had a crushed vertebra in my lower back and cracked
bone in my neck. (Sorry I can't describe these any better). What I know
from here on I got mostly from Nels Fendrich, who was a Beech engineering
test pilot. Nels finished up the certification flying in the Bonanza
after Harry was killed. Anyway, Nels told me the accident was caused by
the large (outboard) right hand landing gear door somehow sucking open
during the dive, tearing off the rib the door was hinged to and then the
wing failed at the rib. The plane then violently rolled to the right and
the left wing failed. The tail then came off and what was left of the
fuselage started tumbling through the air. Harry Reiter fell clear of the
fuselage, but his parachute never opened, so they assumed he was knocked
unconscious.

As far as I know, there was never anything about the accident being caused by tail flutter and I talked to Ralph Harmon, the Project Engineer, and Jerry Gordon, the Chief Aerodynamist, about it. The way I have described it is the way they thought it happened. If you would like to get Nels' opinion, his address is: Nels Fendrich, 907 Drexel Hills Blvd., New Cumberland, Pa. 17070. The last I knew of Ralph Harmon, he was Vice President and Chief Engineer of Mooney Aircraft. I have lost track of Jerry Gordon.

I seldom fly any more, though I did have some fun flying a Bensen gyrocopter out in the desert. I work as an engineer for TRW and my recreation is sailing.

Thanks for the information on the twin Bonanza. I knew Dave Peterson and he gave me a ride in the plane. It was a good airplane.

If I can help you in any way, please let me know. The best of luck to you, Doctor.

Sincerely,

Robert R. King

March 9, 1972

Mr. Larry A. Ball
8407 Peach Tree Lane
Wichita, Kansas 67207

Dear Larry:

    I spent much of last evening snuggled up with
"Those Incomparable Bonanzas," which arrived yesterday.
What a nostalgic binge!

    Hope Frank Hedrick hasn't banished you to Siberia
for running my picture the way you did!

    Incidentally, as I recall it (26 years ago!) that
picture of me on xvii was taken during the day and night
I spent flying one of the experimental Bonanzas on that
accelerated service test program you described on page 22.
I think I had to wear the chute for that reason. I still
remember the night operations vividly. The triangular
route from Beech to Hutchinson, Anthony and back to Beech
was my first contact "in depth" with that remarkable airplane. We'd find the Beech field in the dark by turning
on the landing lights as we came up on the single red
light on the water tank, then circle to the south, kick
the tail left and right, until the runway-edge reflectors
popped up out of the black. No lights in those days!

    That, by the way, was on December 2, 1946 in NX-80300.
I'd flown NX-80040 July 5-6, 1946 with Harry Reiter, Beech's
wonderful test pilot, whose death in that dive test you
mention later on. I think 80040 later was the plane--

● Member: International Council of Aircraft Owner and Pilot Associations

Mr. Larry A. Ball
March 9, 1972
Page 2

modified slightly--used by Odom and Mack.

Where did you find that picture of me? If the negative is still in Beech's files, could you spirit a print to me without revealing the insidious plot to Hedrick or Bill Robinson?

Many thanks for the copy. Hope to mention it in The PILOT, on the off chance that some people besides me and the ABS still think the Bonanza was the greatest thing since Howard Hughes' bra.

Best,

Max/s

Max Karant
Senior Vice President

THIS LETTER WAS DICTATED BY
MR. KARANT AND TRANSCRIBED
AFTER HE LEFT THE OFFICE

16301 Plummer Street
Sepulveda, California 91343

May 14, 1973

Dr. B. J. McClanahan
St. James Mercy Hospital
411 Canisteo Street
Hornell, N. Y. 14843

Dear Dr. McClanahan:

I enclose a copy of a letter I just received from Nels Fendrich, the
former Beech Test Pilot who finished the certification flying on the
Bonanza. As Nels says, we had three accidents prior to the one I
parachuted out of. No one was injured in these three accidents, though
it was mighty close.

If you have any more questions, just write to Nels or me.

Sincerely,

Bob

Robert R. King

286

This is a letter written to the survivor of the experimental Bonanza crash, Bob King. It was written by Nels Fendrich, an experimental test pilot who took over after Harry Reiter was killed. For ease of reading, I have transcribed it from his handwritten letter.

May 8, 1973

Dear Bob:

My apologies for not writing sooner — I did receive your letter in February with the write up about the Bonanza accident and somehow didn't send you any comments I might have had — in general, it is entirely correct, of course, and I can still remember running thru the factory to get to Gaty's office that morning when you called on the phone. You may not recall it but the CAA inspector — can't remember his name now — was with me since we were waiting for you and Harry to return with the airplane to proceed with more of the official CAA test.

In reading your second letter to Dr. McClanahan I have a couple of points which should be of interest concerning the why of the accident. As you mentioned, the landing gear doors bent down during the first flight — and they bent down just as you got to the Vg dive speed — I well remember this particular point because it stuck in my mind that night. I couldn't figure the coincidence of the doors bending at that airspeed and it wasn't until after the accident that I suddenly realized the reason for it — many's the time since that I have wished I could have been thinking more clearly on the day of your first dive. Anyway I remember Harmon and the engineers looking over the doors and figuring a quick fix with the stiffeners which they riveted on a new set of doors. After the accident, when I was in the hangar where the wreckage had been hauled, I noticed again the identical door bending in spite of the stiffeners and you had told me that the thing happened again at the airspeed you were shooting for. It suddenly occurred to me what would always happen at that airspeed and that was of course when Harry would have started his pull out. This naturally placed a heavy down load on the gear retracting mechanism and caused the gear to sag down thereby opening the doors to the slipstream.

As I stood there I recall Jack Gaty came in the hangar and I told him right then what I figured had caused the two occurrences. The experts figured that the turbulent air over the tail caused the tail surfaces to fail — this caused a nose over condition and shortly thereafter the wings came off "downward relative to the fuselage which must have pitched violently down."

You may not recall the sequence of events after that day — anyway, they decided to get a second airplane ready and I said we should have a micro-switch installed on each door which would lite a lite on the panel if the doors started open at all. In addition it was decided to lower the dive speed somewhat (220 I think) and have only pilot in the airplane — plus a chase plane in the form of a Model 18 twin with Vern Carstens flying it.

All this was done and off we went. I started the dive and quit some time before reaching 200, the one lite came on — so down we went — tightened up the mechanism to close more tightly and back up again. This time everything went okay and that was that.

However, they did put an "up" latch on the gear mechanism so that a pull out would not cause any sagging of the gear mechanism — (done later). I understand that they made several dives after I left using a radio controlled airplane with no one in it. I got started in that prior to leaving and had a few hair-raising flights in the airplane with Don Walters to learn to take it off and land it from a Beech 18, I think you remember Don Walters. Wonder what ever happened to him?

I guess you recall the accident to the four engine — 2 prop airplane in which Joe Drum was killed. This happened shortly after I left and was the result of a situation I didn't like and tried to get Herb Rawdon to change — it had to do with the free — wheeling clutches on the engines and the impossibility of starting engines in the event of loss of electrical power. They lost their electrical power and inadvertently turned off all the ignition switches also — the 4 engines stopped — the props freewheeled and there was no way to get them started even if the ignition was turned back on.

Well, Bob, I hope all this is of some help, although naturally you have all the facts correct as they happened. I don't fly much — occasionally fly a Piper Cherokee 180 in a flying club but that's all. Frankly with the new FAA regs and the restrictions on where you can go it isn't quite the fun it used to be.

Marie has been fighting a serious blood disorder since last August and finally now as of the past two weeks she has improved considerably. We are optimistic and her morale is really great which

Beechcraft Twin Quad (Model 34), 20 passenger transport.

After the crash, January 17, 1948.

has been a big factor in the results the doctors have had. She goes in the hospital for treatments every 3-4 weeks — we hope that will spread out gradually but we know it will have to keep on. Our family is fine. To recap briefly — our son is married (9 months) and lives about 15 miles away — Cynthia is married (2½ years) and is in the process of moving from Kansas City to the Washington, D.C. area —Mary (18) is a student at Eastman School of Music.

All this brings back a lot of memories about our days with Beech — do your remember you and I on an engine cooling test on the Model 35 when we heard a noise and came back with a completely broken crankshaft. Then the time Harry, Ralph and Jerry Gordon threw a blade of the forged magnesium prop off coming back from Kansas City — that Harry lost all the accessory gears on the first Continental engine on the Model 35 on takeoff.

Do you recall the tests on the D18C, trying to get the airplane to perform on single engine — we went all the way to Rochester, N.Y. to get close to sea level altitude to try to get better results — to no avail. I can still see the waves on Lake Ontario as we would go out about 20 miles and get down about 10 feet off the water, then lower the gear, shut off one engine and let it windmill and start to climb. What a bunch of nuts.

Well, Bob, that's about the wind up — thanks for your letters and sorry to be so late replying. Our best regards to Faith from your eastern friends,

— Nels Fendrich

A Two Product Line Beechcraft D18S Twin Beeches and the A35 Bonanza — 1949.

May 21, 1973

B. J. McClanahan, M. D.
The St. James Mercy Hospital Laboratory
411 Canisteo Street
Hornell, New York 14843

Dear Mac:

It was great hearing from you.

Actually, it could be possible that King, Karant, McClanahan and Ball
are all correct in part. When I decided to mention the accident in
"Those Incomparable Bonanzas" I discussed it with several old hands of
great competence in aerodynamics and structures at Beech. I found a
difference of opinion still exists today! That is the reason I did not
go into great detail in attempting to explain the accident.

The original story I heard many years ago when I first joined Beech, had
this sequence of events:

1. The landing gear door sucked open.

2. This caused damage to the wing rib, allowing the wing upper skin in
    that area to deform (popping rivets, etc.). The upper skin might
    also have failed rivets and changed contour just from the sudden
    high wing internal air pressure.

3. At this high speed, the air flow over the tail was so disturbed that
    violent flutter was set up, the counter balances were thrown from
    the surfaces, and instantly the surfaces and tail left the airplane.

4. The ensuing high negative G-Loads caused the wings to fail immediately.

All of the above could have happened in a very few seconds and appear to
have happened almost instantaneous.

The following supports the "Flutter" theory:

1. King mentions no pull out before or during wing failure. Without some
    appreciable "G" Loading, it is difficult to imagine the wing failing
    because of damage to one rib.

2. The aerodynamics people were never able to even come close to duplicating a condition which would open a landing gear door in a dive, and the structures people were unable to force deformation of a door to the extent required and with the estimated pressures. (If we accept the above, then, it would have been high speed flutter alone that caused the accident.)

I have no favorite theory, but you can see from the original account I heard, that it would be possible for all of the published accounts to be correct in part.

Incidentally, shortly after "Those Incomparable Bonanzas" was released I received a nice letter from Mr. King and he enclosed a complete written account of the accident which I may use at the next revision.

Best personal regards,

Larry A. Ball
Vice-President-General Manager

P.S. You are correct in your analysis that the caption on page 199 is wrong. This was one of a very few pictures I captioned hurriedly and at the last minute before going to press. Look again though, and tell me if it might not be a 1969 V35A-"TC"?

LAB/bb

June 5, 1973

Mr. Robert R. King
16301 Plummer Street
Sepulveda, California 91343

Dear Bob:

Thanks once more for the additional information which you supplied me in the form of a xerox copy from your friend Nels Fendrich. This was extremely interesting. I had never heard of the other three accidents in the Bonanza which Nels mentioned in his letter.

Nels must have had an awful lot of faith in the Bonanza design to go ahead and complete the dive test after Harry Reiter was killed and you almost. I was also interested in his comments about testing the Beech twin D-18C over Lake Ontario at Rochester, New York. You fellows certainly had more nerve and courage than myself.

At this point in the history of private aviation, I am beginning to feel like Nels states about with the new FAA regs, it is going to be more and more difficult (and expensive) to fly one's own plane. Aviation safety is now at an all time high, but at the same time the FAA is insisting on more and more stringent rules. Let's hope we won't be phased out completely by government regulations.

If you ever happen to be in this part of New York State, be sure and stop in for a chat about Bonanzas.

Best wishes.

Sincerely,

B. J. McClanahan, M. D.

BJM:maf

294

First Concept of Beech Bonanza

This original artist dwg. made from sketches and dwgs. made by Ralph Harmon. This dwg and other material was presented to Beech Management.

The Bonanza project was approved with R. Harmon in charge of design.

1944

"This is the drawing that Walter Beech looked at on my desk and said, 'By God, that's what we should build!' " Ralph Harmon.

*Ralph M. Harmon
& Associates, Inc.*

Consultants
Aviation
Marine
512-367-5864
512-758-5961

Ralph M. Harmon, Pres.
Res. 113 Briarwood
Kerrville, TX
78028

January 17,1989

Mr. Larry Ball
7517 Palais Court
Indianapolis
Indiana, 46278

Dear Larry:

I am pleased to hear that you are thinking about a updating your fine
book about the Bonanza. You did such a fine job on the original, I'm
sure any thing you do for the future editions will be first class
also.

A few comments about the material enclosed.

The story published in the Western Bonanza Society periodical is their
attempt to transcribe a tape, lousy speaking, misspelled words etc.
However, it does tell the story as accurately as possible on how the
Bonanza got started and some of the competition from various factions
who sought to influence the product. It is hard to realize how
difficult it was at times to ward off the old·time thinking that was
so well entrenched at the time. Today, it seems so innocuous to have
such things as tricycle gear, loud speakers, nose wheel steering,
bells instead of klaxon horns and the like. Also, the fact only the
pro-pilots could fly airplanes and the sales people, engineers, and
business types were off limits. These pro-pilots were self serving
protectionist and was a tough bunch to compete against in that day and
age at Beech.

Included are copies of various documents, many of which may not be of
interest in your program. They are included for documentation
purposes only. They tend to verify my activity in the Bonanza and
other aircraft plus how I was positioned in the Beech hierarchy during
those exciting days. They may have little or no value to what you are
interested in. Some of them verify what I said in the talk to WBS.
I have a number of old Beech Logs, photographs, brochures, news
releases etc. on the various aircraft that I was involved in at Beech
and the other companies. But, this material is basically about the
birth of the Bonanza a little about the flavor of the times.

I honestly believe that had I not been bull headed, tough, stubborn and dictatorial about controlling the design of the Bonanza you and I would not be communicating on this matter today. I stood alone on many design issues but Walter Beech, Ted Wells and for some time Jack Gaty usually backed me up. I was over ruled on very few issues. The low drag wing was the only major one I lost on and it proved to be that I was correct since that wing design parameters were given to Al Mooney who had the courage to use it as well as Piper and others in later years. The Bonanza is good but it could have been a little better had we built it as proposed. It would have been a good seven miles per hour faster even with spattered bugs on it.

I just got a call to go to California on a consulting project and having to put this together in a hurry. Look it over, use any part that you want. I may have a little more when I learn more about what you might be interested in.

I have been writing some of my experiences in the aviation business starting back when I built my first airplane in Greewood in the early thirties on up through Beech, Cessna, McDonald, Mooney and my consulting business. So far I am only up to about the time I went to Beech in 1939. There is a lot more to be done.

Good luck.

Sincerely

Ralph M. Harmon

Harmon Enterprises

Consultants
Aviation
Marine
512-367-5864
512-758-5961

Ralph M. Harmon
Res. 113 Briarwood
Kerrville, TX
78028

June 18,1990

Mr. Larry A. Ball
7517 Palais Center
Indianapolis
IN 46278

Dear Larry:

Enclosed herewith are two black and white photos identified as # 1 and #2.

Photo #1. Foreground, Harry Reiter and Jerry Gordon, just after putting the aircraft in a small field just across Central Ave from Beech and slightly east of the old school house on the north east corner of the intersection. The head showing between Harry and Jerry is Virgil Fisher, a technician who worked in B40 at that time. Virgil was later in the model 34 crash and was seriously injured.

This incident was the result of one of the 7 hour Continental engines we were plagued with during flight test development in the early days. We had a shuttle service using Model 18's hauling engines back and forth between ICT and MSK.

This particular day, I was with Harry in the right seat for some kind of flight. We were about to taxi north out of B40 and I saw Jerry coming towards us. I said to Harry,"this flight is more in Jerry"s bailiwick", I got out, Jerry got in and I went back to engineering and looked out the north window and there was the airplane on the ground north of the plant. A good case of delegating on my part.

Photo #2. Left to right, Ralph Harmon, Jerry Gordon and Harry Reiter. We just missed doing this little performance in front of our competitor, Navion, by about 30 minutes. We had been to MKC to the CAA on the final certification matters on the 35. On the MKC airport as we taxied in there was two Navion's on tour with evidently two more of those 7 hour engines scattered apart on the floor. When we took off we did the most spectacular climb out capable with 185 hp for the Navion crew to witness.. Went over to Kansas City, Kansas for something and did another one for good measure. Enroute to ICT I was flying at 8,000 and all hell broke loose about 30 minutes later, Harry took over and landed the airplane after a board meeting on board discussing whether to

bail out. We had very limited elevator control left. I started
out the door with a chute on and came back in and inquired
whether that trip was really necessary, we experimented with the
elevator control some more and decided to go ahead and land.
There was about a 25 mile and hour wind blowing on the ground.

So goes airplane development.

Please return the originals. I will write the above story in my
book. Feel free to use any on the above comments if you desire.

Sincerely.

Ralph M. Harmon

From left to right, Ralph Harmon, Jerry Gordon, and Harry Reiter — July 26, 1946.

Harry Reiter and Jerry Gordon.

Beech Aircraft Corporation
Wichita, Kansas 67201
U. S. A.

March 18, 1982
AB-82-36

Mr. Larry A. Ball
INDIANA BEECHCRAFT, INC.
Indianapolis International Airport
P. O. Box 41606
Indianapolis, IN 46241

Dear Larry:

On March 25, 1982 a Bonanza V35B will roll out of the Beech factory with a special place in history. This Bonanza celebrates 35 years of continuous production for one of the most popular and enduring single-engine airplanes ever produced. Enclosed is a sketch of the paint scheme and interior of this very special Bonanza.

The 35th Anniversary Bonanza has an important marketing mission to accomplish during the remainder of this year. It will be on display at trade shows and conventions this summer, but its primary goal is to help you sell more airplanes by attracting qualified Bonanza prospects to your facility. The most likely environment might be an open house, grand opening, local aviation day, etc. The airplane will be used for static display only. However, the accompanying Bonanza representative will be ready to help meet demonstration requirements in your airplanes.

This program has great sales and public relations potential for all of us. I encourage you to take advantage of this by calling me at (316) 681-8550 and scheduling the 35th Anniversary Bonanza to be at your facility this year.

Sincerely,

Kenneth Mikolajchak
Associate Sales Manager
Bonanzas

KM:dk

Enclosure

A Raytheon Company

301

Aviation Hall of Fame enshrines Walter H. Beech

Beech Aircraft co-founder joins aviation pioneer ranks

Mrs. O. A. Beech with a reproduction of the Walter H. Beech portrait which now hangs in the Aviation Hall of Fame. The portrait was done by Milton Caniff.

Vol. 32   **August 4, 1977**   **No. 14**

During ceremonies held in Dayton, Ohio, July 23, Walter H. Beech, co-founder of Beech Aircraft Corporation, was enshrined into the prestigious Aviation Hall of Fame.

At the formal affair, Mrs. O. A. Beech, chairman, accepted the gold medal award in behalf of her late husband.

Joining four other outstanding aviation pioneers inducted this year, Lawrence D. Bell, Will Rogers, James McDonnell and Alan Shephard, Mr. Beech was chosen by a 125-member nominating board "for his outstanding contributions as a pilot, instructor, practical aeronautical engineer; and for co-founding Travel Air Manufacturing Company and later Beech Aircraft Corporation which designed, manufactured and sold high-quality, top performing aircraft for private, commercial and military use that were generally unexcelled in their class; and for his career-long advocacy and activities touching almost every facet of privately-owned and business aircraft use."

During the ceremonies, Mr. Beech was presented to the organization by his long-time friend Lt. Gen. James H. 'Jimmy' Doolittle, USAF (ret.). The text of General Doolittle's presentation speech, a glowing tribute to Mr. Beech, follows:

"I come to present the first pioneer tonight with great personal pleasure for I have known him for over half a century. I flew and raced his airplanes and remained a close friend for the rest of his life.

"His story is, indeed, the story of the American way of life: success in a chosen field by a dedicated individual who prepares himself well for it and continues to give that extra effort to assure the excellence of his achievements and who, in the end, gives far more to the world than he takes from it.

"As a farm boy, growing up near Nashville, Tenn., Walter Herschel Beech began his aeronautical activities at the age of 14 when he built a crude glider. His takeoff down the sloping barn roof was suddenly ended when he smashed into a nearby barbed wire fence, and by the licking he received when his mother discovered he had used her finest sheets to cover his glider's wings and tail.

"But the boy was destined to become an airman and his career took a giant step forward after he moved to Minneapolis. There, he and a friend bought a wrecked Curtiss Pusher biplane. After they put it back into flying condition, Beech made his first solo flight in July, 1917 from a pasture outside the city. From that moment on, flying became one of the most important things in his life.

"After the United States declared war on Germany in 1917, he enlisted in the aviation section of the Army Signal Corps because he was by then an experienced pilot and engine expert. He was assigned to famous Kelly Field in Texas to instruct flying cadets.

"After the war, he remained an instructor until he resigned his commission in 1920 and joined the barnstormers touring the country try-

continued on page 4

King Air to explore Egyptian deserts

A Beechcraft Super King Air equipped with remote sensing equipment and specialized electronics has been purchased by the Egyptian government to continue water, uranium and other resource exploration in the Sinai and Egyptian deserts begun by American satellites.

Scheduled for delivery in mid 1978, the Beechcraft Super King Air's mission will also be to spot areas in the desert which are arable. This information will be used to move nomadic tribes to these areas before the agricultural potential in their current locations is exhausted.

"This is a new concept in the exploration of natural resources and demography and to our knowledge, is the first time a general aviation airplane will be used for such a purpose," said M. G. Neuburger, senior vice president-International Division.

Photographs taken from the ERTS-1 and Landsat satellites have revealed the existence of water, oil, uranium and other minerals in the Egyptian Sahara and Sinai Peninsula. Preliminary indications show enough water in certain areas to carry out successful irrigation operations.

Also equipped with sophisticated cameras, the Beechcraft Super King Air will follow up these satellite pictures with more detailed information for exploration by the Egyptian government.

This Friday all Beechcraft employees will receive detailed reports on the financial condition of the company's retirement and insurance plans.

A 1974 federal law called the Employee Retirement Income Security Act (ERISA), requires that these reports be made each year.

Beechcrafters are assured that their various benefit plans are in excellent condition, including retirement, group insurance and dental plans. Group insurance shows the impact of rising costs, however the company is currently absorbing those extra costs.

Although you may wish to read the financial reports, no action is required on your part.

Medal presented to Mrs. Beech in commemoration of Mr. Beech's enshrinement.

The following correspondence was received by Frank E. Hedrick, president, from a White House executive staff member.

Hedrick had sent the president's energy chief, James R. Schlesinger, a summary of the energy-saving programs being undertaken at Beech.

Mr. James R. Schlesinger has asked me to reply to your letter and to thank you for providing him with a summary of the energy conservation programs initiated by the Beech Aircraft Corporation.

He was most pleased to note that as a result of your energy conservation programs that it requires 24 percent less energy to manufacture a Beechcraft airplane than it did in 1972, as well as the major projects you are considering for future implementation. The Beech Aircraft Corporation's operations and your customer energy education efforts are commendable and accent the President's belief that through the cooperation and self-sacrifice of all Americans we can resolve our Nation's energy problems.

Pleased be assured that your comments and views will be seriously reviewed as part of the ongoing effort on behalf of the President to solicit the views and opinions of the American public relative to the formulation of future energy policies and initiatives.

Your interest in taking the time to write and share your views are appreciated and Mr. Schlesinger extends his best regards to you and the employees of the Beech Aircraft Corporation.

Preston Trophy winners named

Winners of the BEC's elite 'Preston Trophy' for skill on the skeet range was the team consisting of (l-r) Neil Carlson (884), Lachen Dersi (guest), Bennett Grate (90), Eileen (Mrs. Jim) Dolbee and Jim Dolbee (90).

Aviation Hall of Fame selects Mr. Beech

continued from page 1

ing to eke a living out of coaxing the curious but cautious public into the air. He flew war surplus Jennies in almost every state of the union. Through this experience, often perilous and usually financially disastrous, he learned a lot about the needs of private flying, which served him in good stead in later years.

"In 1921, Beech joined the Swallow Airplane Manufacturing Company in Wichita and soon convinced its president, Jake Moellendick, that the best way to sell the Swallow was not to let it sit on the ground for people to paw over, but to show them what it could really do in the air. Before long, Beech was winning prize money and trophies at air meets throughout the midwest. And sales of Swallow airplanes soared.

"He was so successful that in 1923 he became Swallow's vice president and general manager. But in 1924, after a controversy arose over whether wood or metal tubing should be used in the fuselage of a new Swallow, Beech resigned and he and a group of mavericks eagerly set out to form their own company to show the world what a good airplane really was."

Highlights of Mr. Beech's career as one of the world's outstanding aviation pioneers from his days with Travel Air Company through the maturation of Beech Aircraft Corporation were traced in a narrative film shown during General Doolittle's presentation.

As a president and general manager of Travel Air Manufacturing Company, Walter Beech set out to create aircraft with superior performance. Travel Airs were the proof of Mr. Beech's success. A host of records were captured by his aircraft during the 1920's. Celebrities from all over the country became Travel Air owners as the company became the world's largest builder of private aircraft.

During the twenties Travel Airs twice won the Ford Reliability Tour (once in 1926, in instrument flight conditions); a Travel Air made the first commercial flight from California to Hawaii and a Travel Air won the Dole Air Derby piloted by Art Goebel and his navigator, William Davis; Louise Thaden flew her Travel Air to victory in Women's Derby of the 1929 National Air Races.

1929 was also the year the Travel 'Mystery Ship' was introduced. The Beech designed racer outflew the day's military pursuit aircraft to win the first Thompson Trophy Race. Later, another Mystery S set over 200 records in the air.

In 1932 Mr. and Mrs. Walter H. Beech founded Beech Aircraft Company and set out to build the finest cabin airplane in the world. The Beechcraft Model 17 cabin biplane far exceeded all expectations. Records again began to fall to a Beech designed product and people all over the world took note of the revolutionary 'Staggerwing'.

In 1937 Beech Aircraft introduced the twin-engine Model 18 'Twin Beech' and almost overnight Twin Beeches were being flown in 23 countries. As WWII threatened, the Chinese ordered Staggerwings for ambulance planes and Model 18s for trainers and light bombers to fight the Japanese invaders.

During WWII Beech Aircraft provided a number of modified Model 17s and Model 18s for military use and produced the plywood AT-10 twin-engine trainer to save precious metal. The company also built parts for troop-carrying gliders and A26 'Invaders'. By war's end, Beech Aircraft had delivered 7,400 aircraft to the military and had won five of the coveted "E" Awards for production efficiency.

Post-war developments at Beechcraft were to concentrate on improving the Model 17 and Model 18 but the big news, soon to break, was the introduction of the Beechcraft Bonanza. The unique V-tail aircraft won its bid for immortality when Captain Bill Odom flew his "Waikiki Beech" Bonanza nonstop from Hawaii to New Jersey.

In 1950, while guiding the company in its efforts to help the U.S. rearm to meet the Korean crisis, Mr. Beech died of a heart attack.

"Certainly Walter Herschel Beech has left a valued legacy to aviation. Through personal determination and creativity, plus the will and spirit of a true pioneer, he set the path for his adventure in the skies. In doing so, he created new kinds of aircraft that opened frontiers and brought the benefits of his efforts to all mankind, earning him a cherished niche in the Aviation Hall of Fame."

Since the founding of the Aviation Hall of Fame in 1972, just 75 aviation pioneers have been enshrined. The group, so honored, ". . . represents the history of flight and includes some who dreamed of its possibilities, some who gave their lives in its cause, some who made it a practical reality, and some who have shown the way to the limitless universe."

Supervisors set Lakeside event

The Wichita Division Supervisors Club will have its annual Lakeside Event, Saturday August 6 at the BEC Lakesite recreational area.

The members-only event will feature games, drawings for prizes, free beer and a steak fry with all the trimmings. Kick off time is at 2:00 p.m.

Use 13th Street entrance.

35th Anniversary Beechcraft Bonanza.

BONANZA AT SUNSET

This picture was taken December, 1965 while we were on our way to Phoenix, Arizona from Lake Powell, Utah. This was one of my last V35 demonstrators, N2008W. I kept this airplane for 600 hours, longer than any other demonstrator.

We were a five plane group on a photo mission for a new brochure of the Bonanza and also one for the Musketeer. Jim Yarnell shot a series of photos that evening. As I recall, he was using up film. We were all low on fuel and low on daylight. Years later I saw this airplane in Logansport, Indiana. At the time it was owned by four flying priests.

This picture has endured for 25 years.

Waikiki Beech in the Smithsonian Air and Space Museum.

Cut-a-way Bonanza located below it was previously on display at the factory.

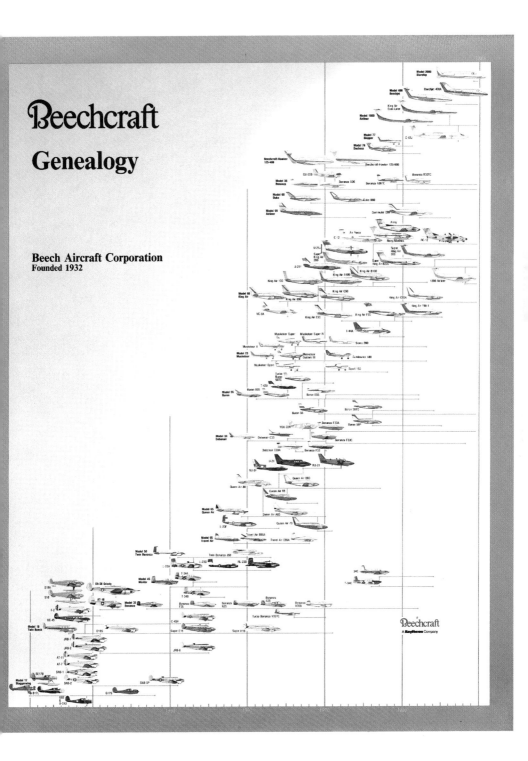

Beechcraft
Genealogy

Beech Aircraft Corporation
Founded 1932

Ohio Aviation, Cincinnati.

Ohio Aviation, Cleveland, Ohio. Now Beckett Enterprises.

Ohio Aviation, Dayton, Ohio. Now Stevens Aviation.

Hartzog Aviation, Rockford, Illinois.

Indiana Beechcraft, Indianapolis, Indiana.

From left to right, Betty Haesloop (wife of then Executive Director of the American Bonanza Society Ralph Haesloop), the author and his wife, Linda, at the Awards Banquet held during the 1967 Beechcraft Sales Spectacular.

1966 V35 Bonanza in Idaho — December, 1966.

Larry Ball and Miss Bonanza of 1968.

From left to right, Air Race Champion Judy Wagner, Mrs. Beech, the author, Judy's husband, Dr. Ellis Wagner, at the 1967 Beechcraft Sales Spectacular.

Bonanza at Aspen, Colorado — December, 1966.

The new C33 Debonair in San Antonio, Texas — August, 1965.

Fred Otnes

Fifty
Years
of
Flight

By GARY WALTHER
Illustrations by FRED OTNES

A 50th anniversary is always a time
for celebration. But, for Beech Aircraft,
Raytheon's newest and largest
subsidiary, it is also a time for
reflection, a chance to look back on a
half century that has seen the
company grow from little more than
the dream of its founders, Walter and
Olive Ann Beech, to a nearly billion-
dollar corporation at the forefront
of general aviation.

Looking over a company history
gives a good picture of the company's
successes and accomplishments, but to
really understand what a company is made
of, and what it stands for, you need to
be in on its birth. You need to meet the
people who laid its foundation. You need to
turn back the clock and try to imagine
what it was like.

By any yardstick, Walter H. Beech could not have chosen a worse moment to launch Beech Aircraft Corporation. It was 1932, and the United States was at the bottom of the Great Depression. More than eight million people were out of work and hundreds of businesses had gone bankrupt since the stock market crash three years before. A man had to be crazy to leave an executive position with Curtiss-Wright Corporation to start manufacturing airplanes from scratch. After all, who had the money to buy them?

But that was Walter Beech's hallmark. Risk whetted his appetite, adversity stiffened his resolve. "We're going to build the best damned airplane ever," he vowed in 1932, "and no near depression is going to stop us."

He defied circumstances that would have given other men pause, and he prevailed. Take, for example, the 1926 Ford Reliability Tour, a grueling 2,575-mile zig-zag air race across the midwest. Just before the seventh leg of the race, a 213-mile dash from Lincoln, Nebraska, to Wichita, Kansas, Beech discovered a leak in the fuel line of his airplane. The gasoline was running out in a stream "as thick as your fingers," he later recalled. He could have repaired the leak and written off that leg. He had already taken five of the first six laps of the competition; he could afford to lose this one.

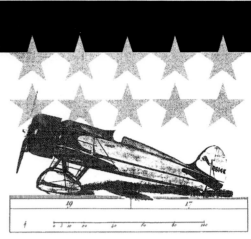

But as he told reporters later, "I was determined to be in Wichita first." And he was. He shot into the city seven minutes ahead of the field with two gallons of gasoline left in the tank, having flown the entire distance at tree-top level with the throttle wide open.

Beech went on to win twelve of the fourteen legs of the race, a performance nothing short of sensational. He was at the peak of his flying career, having won eighteen air races in six years. An admirer summed it all up after the race. Walter Beech had a special combination of determination, daring, and courage, he said. Walter Beech had nerve.

Aviation was just over the horizon when Beech was born in Pulaski, Tennessee, in 1891. Just 12 years later, Orville Wright would make history by piloting the Wright Flyer down a lonely stretch of North Carolina beach. In those days a would-be pilot soloed right from the start. Beech earned his wings in 1914 by rebuilding a wrecked Curtiss Pusher Biplane and towing it back to the airfield where it had gone down. After some brief instructions from the original owner, he strapped himself into the wicker chair that passed for the cockpit and took off.

Beech honed his flying skills as a pilot and flight instructor during World War I. Afterward he bought a war-surplus Jenny and joined the fraternity of hard-driven, daredevil flyers forced out of work by the armistice, who crisscrossed America giving aerobatic demonstrations and earned a living by taking up the stout-hearted for $1 a minute. Those pilots went by many names: gypsy flyers, exhibition flyers, birdmen, barnstormers. More often than not they slept beneath the wings of their planes in whatever pasture they happened to land. It was the era of the aerial stunters, men like "Upside Down" Pangborne, and Lincoln Beachey,

who scooped handkerchiefs off the ground with the wings of his biplane, and Art Goebel, who once flew under the Colorado Street Bridge in Pasadena, California, with a woman standing on each wingtip.

Walter Beech toured all 48 states in his war-surplus Jenny, and also managed to run a charter air taxi business on the side. But the times were changing and Beech knew it. People were growing accustomed to the airplane, and even before the barnstorming days began to wain out in the early 1930s, the age of commercial aviation was beginning. In 1922, Beech parked his Jenny in a pasture and took a job as test pilot and salesman for the Swallow Airplane Manufacturing Company of Wichita.

Wichita was a "boom town" in the 1920s. Since its founding in 1870, the city had ridden the boom-to-bust rollercoaster in cattle, in oil, and even in rabbits, a short-lived enthusiasm promoted by a shady conman named Rajah. Aviation, however, was the boom that would last. Wichita had the right terrain—flat (in fact the city was called the world's largest natural airport). It had the right weather—clear. And it had the right people—besides Walter Beech, two other aviation pioneers, Clyde Cessna

and Lloyd Stearman, were working in the city's fledgling aircraft industry.

This trio would pool their talents in 1925 to start their own aircraft company. By then Beech was a general manager at Swallow, but he ran headlong into the company's rambunctious president, oil-man Jake Moellendick, over aircraft design. Beech believed that airplane fuselages should be built of welded metal tubing, a new idea at the time. Moellendick wanted to continue making them out of wood. Beech resigned. Stearman, who was Swallow's chief designer, went with him, and the two joined forces with Clyde Cessna to form the Travel Air Manufacturing Company.

The first Travel Air plane was built in an old, abandoned planing mill. Beech flew it to victory in the 1925 Ford Reliability Tour as he would the following year. He was flying now because he had to show what Travel Airs could do, and because his winnings kept the company from drowning in red ink. In the 1926 Reliability Tour, Beech flew a Travel Air 4000 monoplane equipped with instruments that permitted blind flying, the first time such a feat had ever been attempted. "Navigation won the race," Beech said afterward, and from then on, the days when pilots would navigate by following a railway line were numbered.

There are old pilots and there are bold pilots, barnstormers used to say, but there are no old, bold pilots. Perhaps with that maxim in mind, Beech hung up his goggles in 1926 and concentrated on the business end of Travel Air. Three years later, the company unveiled the Mystery-S, a sleek, low-wing monoplane, at the National Air Races in Cleveland. The plane showed its flippers to every other entry, whipping around the pylons at 194.9 miles per hour. None other than Jimmy Doolittle said that the Mystery-S was "beyond question, the finest airplane that I have ever flown."

Travel Air was producing 25 percent of all commercial aircraft in America when the company was bought by Curtiss-Wright Corporation in 1929. Beech worked as a vice president in St. Louis and New York, but his spirit was growing restless. He wasn't the sort of man who was comfortable working for anyone but himself.

So, in 1932, Walter Beech set out on what proved to be his grandest challenge. Along with his wife and business partner, Olive Ann, he staked his life savings on founding the aircraft company that still bears his name.

Beech Aircraft Corporation was born amid headlines as Walter Beech announced plans to build a four-place cabin biplane that would fly 200 miles per hour. Impossible, or so the critics thought.

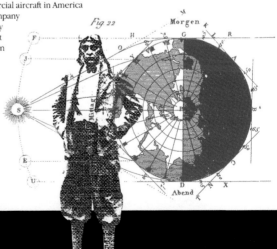

wo months after Beech
Aircraft introduced its first
airplane, the Staggerwing
Model 17, the sleek biplane
flew off with the prestigious Texaco
Trophy Race in Miami. A string of firsts
followed as Beechcrafts won five major
air races in 1936 alone including the
Denver Mile-High Air Race and the
Bendix Transcontinental Speed Dash.
And the winning streak didn't end
there. Beechcrafts continued to pick
up trophies on into the next decade
with victories in the 1937 Unlimited
Race, the 1939 McFadden Cross-Coun-
try Race, and the 1940 On-To-Miami
Air Race.

The wood and wire heroes are gone
now, the barnstorming days a sepia-
tinted memory. Pilots no longer wear
white shirts, bow ties, and plus-fours
as they did in the 1920s, and they are
not likely to swoop down on an open
field, taxi after a wildcat, lasso the ani-
mal, and bring it back in the passenger
seat as Walter Beech did one day while
flying over northern Oklahoma. It's
not easy to sum up a career, but if
there's one expression that exemplifies
Walter Beech's spirit, it's the one that
tumbled from his lips so often during
those early air races, when the chips
were down: "Give it hell and beat
them."

Gary Walther is associate editor of
Americana magazine in New York.

321